DECORATIVE PAINTING

81 Projects & Ideas for the Home

The Home Decorating Institute®

COWLES
Creative Publishing, Inc.

Copyright © 1994 Cowles Creative Publishing, Inc.
5900 Green Oak Drive Minnetonka, Minnesota 55343 • 1-800-328-3895 • All rights reserved • Printed in U.S.A.

Library of Congress Cataloging-in-Publication Data Decorative painting / Home Decorating Institute. p. cm. — (Arts & crafts for home decorating)
Includes index. ISBN 0-86573-365-1 ISBN 0-86573-366-X (softcover) 1. Painting — Technique. 2. Decoration and ornament. I. Home Decorating
Institute (Minnetonka, Minn.) II. Series.   TT835.D43 1994 745.7—dc20   94-7810

CONTENTS

Painting Basics

Painted Designs

Specialty Paints & Glazes

Faux Finishes

Combining Techniques

DECORATIVE PAINTING

Paint finishes add a personal
touch to walls and furnishings.

Decorative painting is a creative way to express your individual style and to give walls, furniture, and room accessories a customized finish. Select from a variety of paint finishes that can be used on plaster, wood, metal, ceramic, and fabric.

Select paint finishes that complement your own decorating style. To contrast with sleek contemporary furnishings, apply a faux granite finish to a piece of sculpture. Use faux rust for a metal lamp that has a Southwestern influence. Use an alabaster finish for traditional crown moldings or a verdigris look for plaster statuary and terra-cotta pots.

Try paint glazes to add visual texture. For walls, you may want a mottled finish in tone-on-tone colors. Or make a bolder statement with strié walls in a deep, rich color.

Water-soluble paints of latex and acrylic are used for all the techniques in this book, to make the cleanup easier and to protect the environment. To achieve the different finishes, various paint mediums are often used to either thin or thicken the paints and to extend their drying time.

Painting
Basics

TYPES OF WATER-BASED PAINT

A wide variety of paint is available from paint supply stores and craft stores. Each type has advantages that make it especially suitable for certain kinds of painting. All of the following are water-based, making cleanup easy with soap and water. Water-based paints are also safer for the environment than oil-based paints.

Latex paint is fast drying and durable. In addition to the wide range of premixed colors, latex paint can be custom-mixed by a paint professional. It is available in various finishes, from flat latex for a matte appearance to high-gloss latex with maximum sheen. Low-luster latex enamel paint, sometimes referred to as eggshell enamel, has some sheen and provides good coverage; semigloss has a bit more sheen. The glossier the paint, the more durable it is. Packaged in pints, quarts, and gallons (0.5, 0.9, and 3.8 L), latex paint is suitable for general use in small and large jobs.

Latex paint contains acrylic or vinyl resins or a combination of both. Latex paints of acrylic resins are the highest quality, with vinyl-acrylic blends next in quality, followed by paints consisting solely of vinyl resins. High-quality paints may cost significantly more, but they provide an even, complete coverage and wear longer.

Aerosol acrylic paints offer excellent coverage and are fast drying. They can be applied quickly and easily without leaving brush marks and are especially convenient for painting textured surfaces that are difficult to paint with a paintbrush. Aerosol acrylic paints are available in a variety of finishes, from matte to high gloss. To protect the environment, select an aerosol paint that does not contain harmful propellants like fluorocarbons or methylene chloride.

Craft acrylic paint contains 100 percent acrylic resins. Generally sold in 2-oz., 4-oz., and 8-oz. (59, 119, and 237 mL) bottles or jars, these premixed acrylics have a creamy brushing consistency and give excellent coverage. They should not be confused with the thicker artist's acrylics used for canvas paintings. Craft acrylic paint can be diluted with water, acrylic extender, or latex paint conditioner (page 10) if a thinner consistency is desired. Craft acrylic paints are available in many colors and in metallic, fluorescent, and iridescent formulas.

Ceramic paints provide a scratch-resistant and translucent finish. They can be heat-hardened in a low-temperature oven to improve the paint's durability, adhesion, and water resistance. Latex and acrylic paints may also be used for painting ceramics, provided the surface is properly primed (page 13).

Fabric paints have been formulated specifically for painting on fabric. To prevent excessive stiffness in the painted fabric, avoid a heavy application; the texture of the fabric should show through the paint. Once the paints are heat-set with an iron, the fabric can be machine washed and dry-cleaned. Acrylic paints can also be used for fabric painting; textile medium (page 11) may be added to the acrylics to make them more pliable on fabric.

Paint mediums, such as conditioners, extenders, and thickeners, are often essential for successful results in decorative painting. Available in latex or acrylic, paint mediums are formulated to create certain effects or to change a paint's performance without affecting its color. Some mediums are added directly to the paint, while others are used simultaneously with paint. Mediums are especially useful for latex and acrylic paint glazes (page 65), in that they make an otherwise opaque paint somewhat translucent.

Latex paint conditioner, such as Floetrol®, was developed for use in a paint sprayer with latex paint, but this useful product is also essential in making a paint glaze for faux finishes. When paint conditioner is added to paint, it increases the drying or "open" time and extends the wet-edge time to avoid the look of overlapping. The mixture has a lighter consistency and produces a translucent paint finish. Latex paint conditioner may be added directly to either latex or acrylic paint.

Acrylic paint extender thins the paint, increases the open time, and makes paint more translucent. It is also used for the characteristic veins of marbled faux finishes. When used for veining, acrylic extender is not mixed with the paint, but rather is placed next to it; the paint and the extender are mingled as a feather is passed through them.

Acrylic paint thickener increases the drying time of the paint while it thickens the consistency. Thickener can be mixed directly into either acrylic or latex paint. Small bubbles may appear while mixing, but they will disappear as the paint mixture is applied. Thickener is used for painting techniques that require a paint with more body, such as wood graining, marbling, and combing.

Textile medium is formulated for use with acrylic paint, to make it more suitable for fabric painting. Mixed into the paint, it allows the paint to penetrate the natural fibers of cottons, wools, and blends, creating permanent, washable painted designs. After the fabric is painted, it is heat-set with an iron.

PRIMERS & FINISHES

PRIMERS

Some surfaces must be coated with a primer before paint is applied. Primers ensure good adhesion of paint and are used to seal porous surfaces so paint will spread smoothly without soaking in. It is usually not necessary to prime a nonporous surface in good condition, such as smooth, unchipped, previously painted wood or wallboard. Many types of water-based primers are available; select one that is suitable for the type of surface you are painting.

Flat latex primer is used for sealing unfinished wallboard. It makes the surface nonporous so fewer coats of paint are needed. This primer may also be used to seal previously painted wallboard before you apply new paint of a dramatically different color. The primer prevents the original color from showing through.

Latex enamel undercoat is used for priming most raw woods or woods that have been previously painted or stained. A wood primer closes the pores of the wood, for a smooth surface. It is not used for cedar, redwood, and plywoods that contain water-soluble dyes, because the dyes would bleed through the primer.

Rust-inhibiting latex metal primer helps paint adhere to metal. Once a rust-inhibiting primer is applied, water-based paint may be used on metal without causing the surface to rust.

Polyvinyl acrylic primer, or PVA, is used to seal the porous surface of plaster and unglazed pottery, if a smooth paint finish is desired. To preserve the texture of plaster or unglazed pottery, apply the paint directly to the surface without using a primer.

Stain-killing primer seals stains like crayon, ink, and grease so they will not bleed through the top coat of paint. It is used to seal knotholes and is the recommended primer for cedar, redwood, and plywood with water-soluble dyes, because it keeps the bleed from these woods from appearing in the paint finish. This versatile primer is also used as the primer for glossy surfaces like glazed pottery and ceramic, making it unnecessary to sand or degloss the surface.

FINISHES

Finishes are sometimes used over paint as the final coat. They protect the painted surface with a transparent coating. The degree of protection and durability varies, from a light application of matte aerosol sealer to a glossy layer of clear finish.

Clear finish, such as water-based urethanes and acrylics, may be used over paint for a durable finish. As with other products, the glossier the finish, the more washable and scratch-resistant. Clear finish is applied with a brush or sponge applicator. Environmentally safe clear finishes are available in pints, quarts, and gallons (0.5, 0.9, and 3.8 L) at paint supply stores and in 4-oz. and 8-oz. (119 and 237 mL) bottles or jars at craft stores.

Aerosol clear acrylic sealer, available in matte or gloss, may be used as the final coat over paint as a protective finish. A gloss sealer also adds sheen and depth to the paint finish for a more polished look. For minimal protection, one light coat is used; several light coats are used for a more durable finish. Avoid applying heavy coats, to avoid dripping or puddling. To protect the environment, select an aerosol sealer that does not contain harmful propellants. Use all aerosol sealers in a well-ventilated area.

TAPES

When painting, use tape to mask off any surrounding areas. Several brands are available, varying in the amount of tack, how well they release from the surface without damaging the base coat, and how long they can remain in place before removal. You may want to test the tape before applying it to the entire project. The edge of the tape should be sealed tightly to prevent seepage.

Painter's masking tape **(a)** is one of several products developed especially for use with paint. Painter's tape **(b)** is a wide strip of brown paper with adhesive along one edge. Stencil tape **(c)** is similar to painter's masking tape; it bonds securely to Mylar® stencils, yet does not damage a painted surface.

PAINT ROLLERS

Paint rollers are used to paint an area quickly with an even coat of paint. Roller pads, available in several nap thicknesses, are used in conjunction with roller frames. Use synthetic or lamb's wool roller pads to apply water-based paints.

Short-nap roller pads **(a)** with ¼" to ⅜" (6 mm to 1 cm) nap are used for applying glossy paints to smooth surfaces like wallboard, wood, and smooth plaster.

Medium-nap roller pads **(b)** with ½" to ¾" (1.3 to 2 cm) nap are used as all-purpose pads. They give flat surfaces a slight texture.

Long-nap roller pads **(c)** with 1" to 1¼" (2.5 to 3.2 cm) nap are used to cover textured areas in fewer passes.

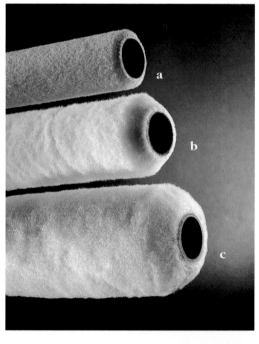

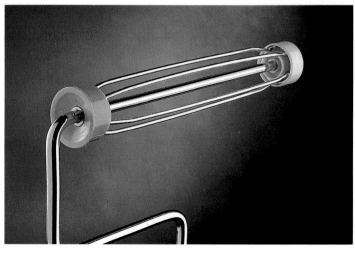

Roller frame is the metal arm and handle that holds the roller pad in place. A wire cage supports the pad in the middle. Select a roller frame with nylon bearings so it will roll smoothly and a threaded end on the handle so you can attach an extension pole.

Extension pole has a threaded end that screws into the handle of a roller frame. Use an extension pole when painting ceilings, high wall areas, and floors.

PAINTBRUSHES & APPLICATORS

Several types of paintbrushes and applicators are available, designed for various purposes. Select the correct one to achieve the best quality in the paint finish.

Synthetic-bristle paintbrushes **(a)** are generally used with water-based latex and acrylic paints, while natural-bristle brushes **(b)** are used with alkyd, or oil-based, paints. If natural-bristle paintbrushes are used with water-based paints, the bristles will bunch together. Although this bunching is undesirable for general painting, natural-bristle paintbrushes are intentionally used with water-based paints to create certain decorative effects. For example, natural-bristle brushes are used to streak a water-based color-washed finish and for dry brushing water-based paints to soften faux wood and strié finishes.

Brush combs **(c)** remove dried or stubborn paint particles from paintbrushes and align the bristles so they dry properly. To use a brush comb, hold the brush in a stream of water as you pull the comb several times through the bristles from the base to the tips. Use mild soap on the brush, if necessary, and rinse well. The curved side of the tool can be used to remove paint from the roller pad.

Stencil brushes are available in a range of sizes. Use the small brushes for fine detail work in small stencil openings, and the large brushes for larger openings. Either synthetic **(d)** or natural-bristle **(e)** stencil brushes may be used with acrylic paints.

Artist's brushes are available in several types, including fan **(f)**, liner **(g)**, and flat **(h)** brushes. After cleaning the brushes, always reshape the head of the brush by stroking the bristles with your fingers. Store artist's brushes upright on their handles or lying flat so there is no pressure on the bristles.

Sponge applicators **(i)** are used for a smooth application of paint on flat surfaces.

Paint edgers with guide wheels **(j)** are used to apply paint next to moldings, ceilings, and corners. The guide wheels can be adjusted for proper alignment of the paint pad.

PREPARING
THE SURFACE

To achieve a high-quality and long-lasting paint finish that adheres well to the surface, it is important to prepare the surface properly so it is clean and smooth. The preparation steps vary, depending on the type of surface you are painting. Often it is necessary to apply a primer to the surface before painting it. For more information about primers, refer to pages 12 and 13.

PREPARING SURFACES FOR PAINTING

SURFACE TO BE PAINTED	PREPARATION STEPS	PRIMER
UNFINISHED WOOD	1. Sand surface to smooth it. 2. Wipe with tack cloth to remove grit. 3. Apply primer.	Latex enamel undercoat.
PREVIOUSLY PAINTED WOOD	1. Clean surface to remove any grease and dirt. 2. Rinse with clear water; allow to dry. 3. Sand surface lightly to degloss and smooth it and to remove any loose paint chips. 4. Wipe with tack cloth to remove grit. 5. Apply primer to any areas of bare wood.	Not necessary, except to touch up areas of bare wood; then use latex enamel undercoat.
PREVIOUSLY VARNISHED WOOD	1. Clean surface to remove any grease and dirt. 2. Rinse with clear water; allow to dry. 3. Sand surface to degloss it. 4. Wipe with tack cloth to remove grit. 5. Apply primer.	Latex enamel undercoat.
UNFINISHED WALLBOARD	1. Dust with hand broom, or vacuum with soft brush attachment. 2. Apply primer.	Flat latex primer.
PREVIOUSLY PAINTED WALLBOARD	1. Clean surface to remove any grease and dirt. 2. Rinse with clear water; allow to dry. 3. Apply primer, only if making a dramatic color change.	Not necessary, except when painting over dark or strong color; then use flat latex primer.
UNPAINTED PLASTER	1. Sand any flat surfaces as necessary. 2. Dust with hand broom, or vacuum with soft brush attachment.	Polyvinyl acrylic primer.
PREVIOUSLY PAINTED PLASTER	1. Clean surface to remove any grease and dirt. 2. Rinse with clear water; allow to dry thoroughly. 3. Fill any cracks with spackling compound. 4. Sand surface to degloss it.	Not necessary, except when painting over dark or strong color; then use polyvinyl acrylic primer.
UNGLAZED POTTERY	1. Dust with brush, or vacuum with soft brush attachment. 2. Apply primer.	Polyvinyl acrylic primer.
GLAZED POTTERY, CERAMIC & GLASS	1. Clean surface to remove any grease and dirt. 2. Rinse with clear water; allow to dry thoroughly. 3. Apply primer.	Stain-killing primer.
METAL	1. Clean surface with vinegar or lacquer thinner to remove any grease and dirt. 2. Sand surface to degloss it and to remove any rust. 3. Wipe with tack cloth to remove grit. 4. Apply primer.	Rust-inhibiting latex metal primer.
FABRIC	1. Prewash fabric without fabric softener to remove any sizing, if fabric is washable. 2. Press fabric as necessary.	None.

SELECTING PAINT COLORS

In color selection, your own likes and dislikes are the most important consideration. Regardless of the current decorating trends, you need to be comfortable with the color scheme. Consider whether you prefer a bold or a subdued look for the overall decorating scheme of the room. Even if you are designing a room that is rather muted, you may want a few brighter accent colors, used sparingly.

In addition to your personal tastes, the colors depend on the type of paint finish, the size of the project, and where it will be used. Paint finishes that include several colors may be a combination of subtle tones or a wide range of colors. You may be painting walls as a backdrop for other furnishings or painting an accent table to be used as a focal point.

Keep in mind that the paint colors you see in the decorating center will look different in your home. Varying lighting conditions, as well as nearby furnishings, can affect the way the paint colors will look. In paint finishes that use a combination of colors, such as a faux mosaic finish, select colors that will work together for the design, and check to see how they will look in the overall scheme of the room.

Before making the final decision on the paint colors, purchase a small quantity of paint in each color and test the paint finish on a large sheet of cardboard. Place it where it will be used in the room, and check it from time to time over a 24-hour period. Notice how the colors work together and how they change in natural and artificial light. If a room is most often used at a particular time of day, look at the color carefully at that time.

Sometimes different colors are used for the base coat and the top coat, as in the glazed finishes on page 65. It is especially important with these paint finishes that you test the painting technique before you make the final color selections.

HOW COLOR AFFECTS DESIGN

Same paint finish can look quite different, depending on the colors selected. For a faux mosaic finish, neutral colors (left), such as gray and gold, produce a simple effect. Add a third color (middle), such as green, and the mosaic design is stronger and more dominant. When several contrasting colors (right), such as black, gray, gold, green, and blue, are combined, the design looks more intricate and makes a bolder statement.

Check samples of paint finishes where they will be used in the room before making the final decision on colors; place a paint sample for a tabletop horizontally on the table, and place a wall sample vertically, so the light strikes the surface correctly. Look at the samples periodically over the next 24 hours to see how the changing light affects the paint finishes. Natural daylight (above, left) has a blue cast at midday and a yellow cast at sunrise and sunset. Incandescent lighting (above, right) has a yellow cast.

Size of the paint samples should be in proportion to how much of each color will be used, such as a large sample in the base coat color and small samples in the accent colors. Several paint chips of a single color can be taped together for a larger sample.

Painted Designs

INSPIRATION
FOR DESIGNS

Nature
*provides both
shape and color
ideas. Autumn leaves
inspire simple free-form designs.*

Inspiring ideas for creating designs can be found by looking closely at the shapes, colors, and textures around you. You may want to paint simple floral patterns that mimic those found in nature. Or adapt a wallpaper design to stencil on coordinating curtains.

To help you decide which designs will work best for you, think about the descriptive words that define your personal tastes and decorating style. For example, if you describe your style as light, airy, and feminine, try a free-form floral design in pastels. For a design that is tailored,

rich, and warm, choose a plaid in deep, inviting colors. For a look that is bright, bold, and clean, you may want to use a contemporary design with strong diagonal lines.

Look through ornamental design books, available at local libraries and bookstores, usually located in the art section. Study the ethnic patterns found on fabrics and accessories, like those on woven rugs and glazed pots. Clip photos from magazines. Even the advertisements in magazines feature the latest colors and patterns in fabrics and furnishings.

Plaid fabric *inspired the bold design for the tabletop at right. The design was painted using evenly spaced rows of painter's masking tape as a guide.*

Wallcovering border *is used for creating the stenciled design on the small wooden chest below.*

Design books *offer a wide selection of designs. Below, a contemporary geometric design appears on a stylized pitcher.*

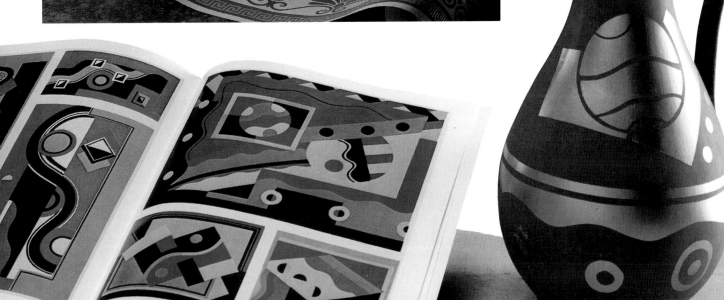

TRANSFERRING DESIGNS

For painted designs, you will often want to mark the design onto the surface after the base coat is applied. Designs can be transferred from wallcoverings, fabrics, books, and any other sources of inspiration (page 22), following a few simple techniques.

The first step in transferring a design is to duplicate it onto paper. To do this, you can cover the design with tracing paper and trace the design lines with a pencil. Hold the covered design up to a light source, such as a sunlit window or a light table, to see the design lines more clearly. A temporary light table can easily be made by placing a light under a glass-top table. As you trace the design, you may want to simplify it for easier painting, omitting fine or unnecessary details. To enlarge or reduce a design, use the grid method to draw the design to scale.

For many designs, a photocopy machine works well to eliminate the need for drawing the design, although any shaded areas in the original design will be copied, and the design will not be simplified. The design may be enlarged or reduced by using a photocopy machine that is set to a larger or smaller percentage of the original.

The design is transferred from the paper to the surface that will be painted, using graphite paper and tracing around the design with a pencil. The graphite lines on the surface mark the placement of the design; they may be erased after the design is painted.

HOW TO ENLARGE OR REDUCE A DESIGN USING THE GRID METHOD

1 Measure length of original design, and decide on the desired finished length; this determines sizes of the grids. For example, a graph paper with ¼" (6 mm) grid can be used to mark original design; for the enlarged design, use paper with ¾" (2 cm) grid to triple the size, as indicated by red lines.

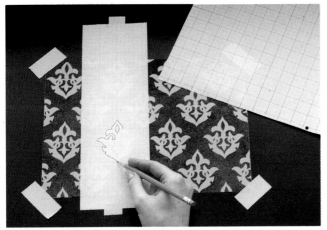

2 Place graph paper over original design; trace design onto graph paper.

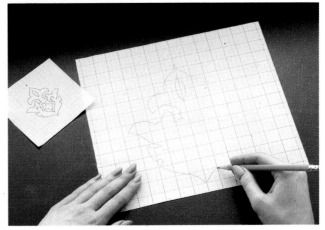

3 Look at original design, and draw design lines within each grid to scale on grid for finished size.

HOW TO ENLARGE A DESIGN USING THE PHOTOCOPY METHOD

1 Draw lines vertically and horizontally through design if finished size of design will no longer fit on a single sheet of paper.

2 Photocopy each area of the design, with the machine set at desired percentage of the original.

3 Continue to make enlarged copies, using the previous copy of each area, until desired size is reached.

4 Trim copies along marked lines; tape sections together to make full-size design.

5 Redraw design lines on tracing paper, if necessary for clarity.

HOW TO REDUCE A DESIGN USING THE PHOTOCOPY METHOD

1 Draw lines vertically and horizontally through design if original size of the design does not fit on single sheet of paper that can be used in the photocopy machine. Cut design apart on marked lines.

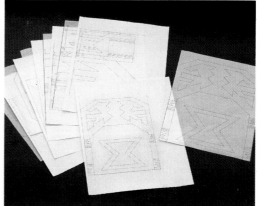

2 Photocopy each area of the design, with the machine set at desired percentage of the original. Darken lines, if necessary.

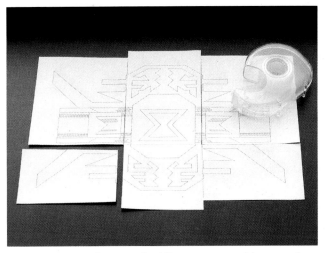

3 Continue to make reduced copies, using the previous copy of each area.

4 Trim copies along marked lines; tape sections together to make full-size design.

HOW TO TRANSFER A DESIGN FOR PAINTING

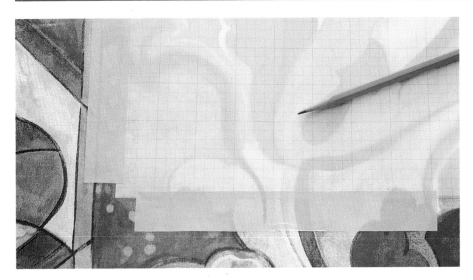

1 Omit this step and step 2 if photocopied design is being used. Place tracing paper over design; work on a lighted surface, if design lines are difficult to see. To keep the design from shifting, tape it to a flat surface; this is especially helpful when tracing designs from fabric.

2 Trace around prominent design lines; simplify design, if desired, by omitting any fine details that would be too difficult or time-consuming to paint. Enlarge or reduce design, if desired, using grid method on page 25.

3 Place photocopied or traced design over a sheet of graphite paper, with graphite side down; tape in desired position on surface to be painted. Outline the design, using pencil, to transfer the design to the surface.

GUIDED DESIGNS

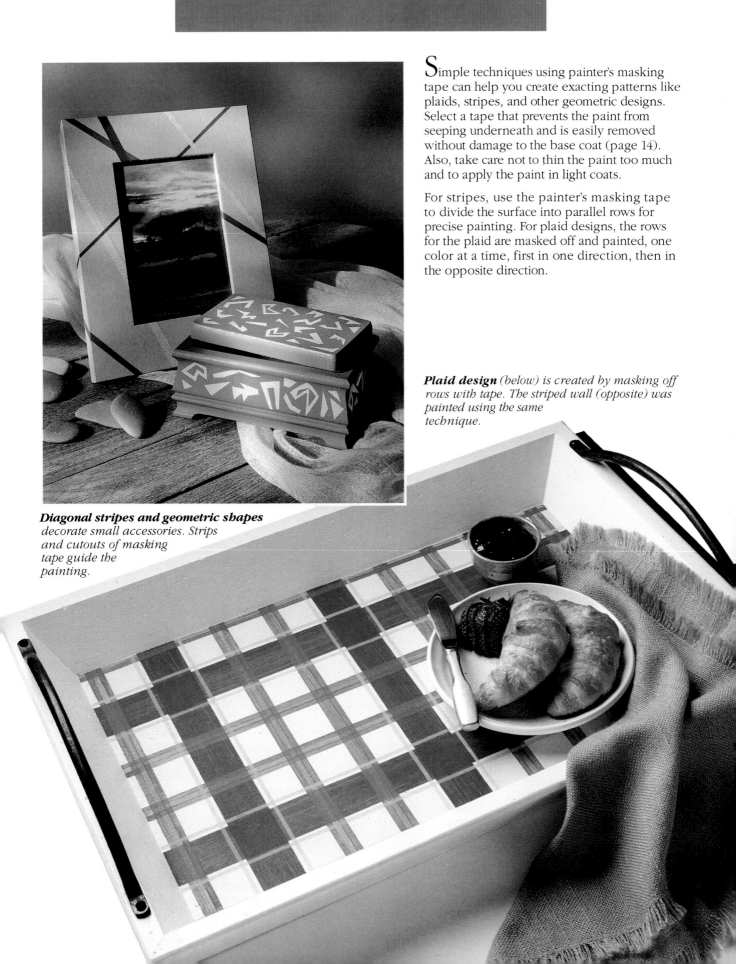

Simple techniques using painter's masking tape can help you create exacting patterns like plaids, stripes, and other geometric designs. Select a tape that prevents the paint from seeping underneath and is easily removed without damage to the base coat (page 14). Also, take care not to thin the paint too much and to apply the paint in light coats.

For stripes, use the painter's masking tape to divide the surface into parallel rows for precise painting. For plaid designs, the rows for the plaid are masked off and painted, one color at a time, first in one direction, then in the opposite direction.

Plaid design *(below) is created by masking off rows with tape. The striped wall (opposite) was painted using the same technique.*

Diagonal stripes and geometric shapes *decorate small accessories. Strips and cutouts of masking tape guide the painting.*

TIPS FOR PAINTING GUIDED DESIGNS

Cut geometric designs from painter's masking tape; apply to the surface over the base coat, pressing edges of tape firmly. Apply paint in a contrasting color; allow paint to dry. Remove the masking tape to reveal designs.

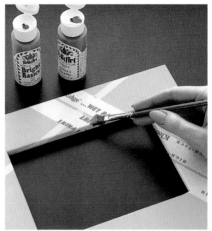

Apply two rows of masking tape to surface over the base coat, pressing edges firmly; apply paint in a contrasting color between rows. Allow paint to dry; remove masking tape.

HOW TO PAINT A STRIPED DESIGN

MATERIALS

- Painter's masking tape in desired width or widths.
- Latex or craft acrylic paints.
- Paintbrush or paint roller.
- Striped fabric, optional, for inspiration.

1 Apply base coat in desired color. Allow to dry.

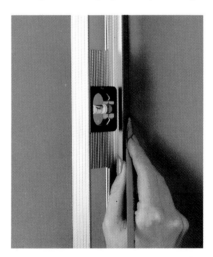

2 Mark a light plumb line, using pencil and carpenter's level, if painting design on a wall. Align the painter's masking tape for first stripe to the plumb line, pressing the edges of the tape firmly.

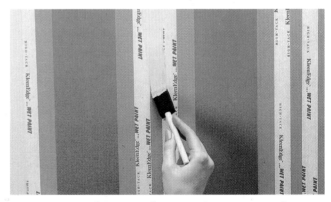

3 Measure and position parallel rows of masking tape for first stripe color, pressing edges firmly. Paint stripes of this color. Allow to dry.

4 Remove masking tape from previous steps. Apply rows of tape for next color; apply paint, and allow to dry. Repeat for any remaining colors.

HOW TO PAINT A PLAID DESIGN

MATERIALS

- Painter's masking tape in desired width or widths.
- Low-luster or mid-sheen latex enamel, for base coat; latex or craft acrylic paints for remaining colors.

- Paintbrush or paint roller, for applying base coat.
- Sponge applicator.
- Plaid fabric, optional, for inspiration.

1 Apply base coat of low-luster or mid-sheen latex enamel in desired color. Allow to dry. For walls, mark vertical plumb line and horizontal level line, using carpenter's level.

2 Apply painter's masking tape of desired widths to the surface in horizontal parallel rows, pressing edges firmly; use plaid fabric as a guide for spacing rows, if desired.

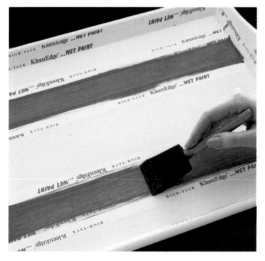

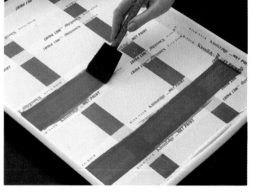

3 Thin paint so it gives translucent look. Apply a light coat of paint in the desired color to areas between the rows of tape. Pull a sponge applicator from one end to the other in a continuous motion, making fine lines in paint that simulate fabric weave. Allow to dry; remove tape.

4 Apply painter's masking tape to surface in vertical parallel rows, pressing the edges firmly. Apply the same paint color in opposite direction, between rows of tape.

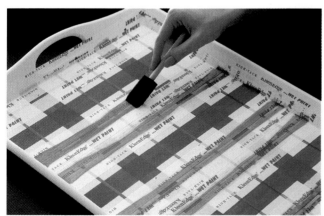

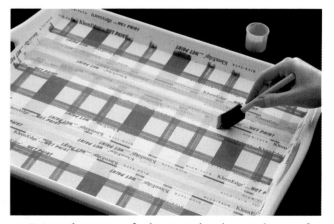

5 Apply horizontal rows of masking tape for next color as in step 2; paint as in step 3. Then apply the masking tape for vertical rows, and apply same paint color.

6 Repeat the process for horizontal and vertical rows of each paint color.

SWIRLED DESIGNS

Swirls of paint created with sweeping brush strokes make interesting designs. The three easy-to-copy designs shown here are created primarily with basic painting tools like artist's brushes, texture rollers, and paint pads. The designs range in scale from small to medium to large.

Paint the designs on walls rather than use wallcoverings, or paint fabrics for unique accent pillows instead of selecting patterned fabrics. For small accessories, use smaller brushes and shorter brush strokes.

Vary the paint colors, selecting different colors for the different brush strokes. Keep in mind that dark and dull colors tend to recede while bright colors and metallic paints tend to advance. Metallic paints, which reflect light, add drama. For painting on fabrics, use the specialty paints intended for textiles, and refer to the painting guidelines on pages 58 and 59 for best results.

When painting, overlap the brush strokes for a more layered, dimensional look. The spaces between the strokes can be varied slightly for interest. Experiment with the paint colors and techniques before you begin the actual project by painting on a large sheet of cardboard or on a remnant of fabric.

MATERIALS

- #4 round artist's brush, for small swirled design.
- #4 fan brush, #2 flat artist's brush, and #4 round artist's brush, for medium swirled design.
- 3" (7.5 cm) flat paintbrush, texture roller, and #4 round artist's brush, for large swirled design.
- Craft acrylic paints.
- Paint tray.

Swirled designs *are made with brush strokes in several colors. These simple designs may be painted on walls (left) as well as on fabrics (below).*

HOW TO PAINT A SMALL
SWIRLED DESIGN

1 Apply the first paint color to surface in slightly curved brush strokes about 4" (10 cm) long and 4" to 6" (10 to 15 cm) apart, using #4 round artist's brush. Allow to dry.

2 Apply the second color in curving brush strokes about 1½" (3.8 cm) long, using the same brush; use less pressure on the paintbrush so strokes are not as wide. Allow some strokes to overlap those of first color. Allow to dry.

3 Apply third color in curving strokes about 1" (2.5 cm) long, using tip of same brush. Allow some strokes to overlap the first color.

HOW TO PAINT A MEDIUM
SWIRLED DESIGN

1 Apply first paint color to surface in brush strokes about 4" (10 cm) long, using fan brush. Allow to dry.

2 Apply the second color through middle of first color in brush strokes about 6" (15 cm) long, using #2 flat artist's brush; vary the position for added interest. Allow to dry.

3 Apply third color in slightly curved brush strokes about 1½" to 2" (3.8 to 5 cm) long, using #4 round artist's brush. Allow to dry.

4 Wet fan brush; blot on paper towel. Separate the bristles into small fingers. Dip into fourth paint color ¼" (6 mm), keeping bristles separated. Apply to surface in short brush strokes, about 1" (2.5 cm) long, applying light pressure.

HOW TO PAINT A LARGE
SWIRLED DESIGN

1 Dilute first paint color, one part paint to two parts water. Using 3" (7.5 cm) paintbrush, apply paint to surface in slightly curved brush strokes, from 7" to 14" (18 to 35.5 cm) long. Allow to dry.

2 Dilute second paint color, one part paint to one part water; spread a thin layer in paint tray. Apply paint to texture roller; blot onto paper, then roll onto surface, overlapping the brush strokes from step 1. Allow to dry.

3 Apply third color in curving brush strokes about 6" to 12" (15 to 30.5 cm) long, using #4 round artist's brush; overlap the brush strokes from step 1. Allow to dry.

4 Apply fourth color in pairs of short brush strokes, using #4 artist's brush; overlap the edges of the strokes from step 1.

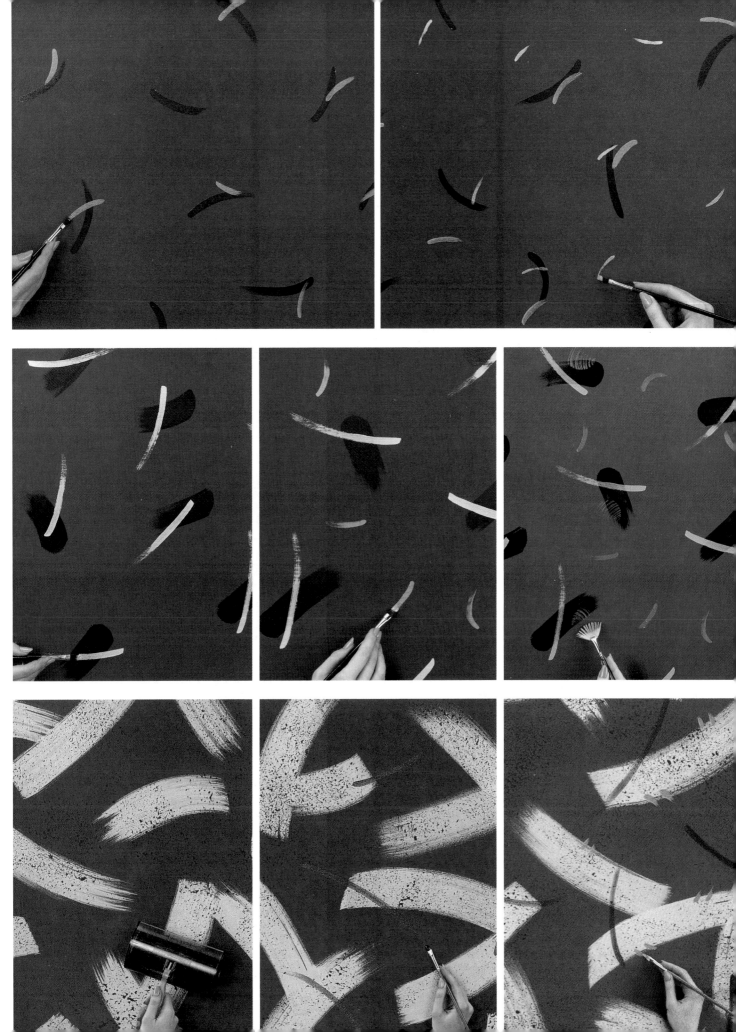

STAMPED DESIGNS

Use a basic stamping technique to create random designs. The paint was applied to the three designs shown here with everyday items like strips of cardboard, triangular makeup sponges, wooden blocks, a spaghetti lifter, and a bottle cork.

The coordinating designs are variations on a theme, and range in scale from small to medium to large. Select your favorite design, or use all three. When stamps are used to create several designs, you may choose to use the same colors, but in different ways. For example, the background color of one design may be used for one of the stamps in another design.

Experiment with the colors and the techniques on a large sheet of cardboard or on a remnant of fabric before you start the actual project. For painting on fabrics, refer to the tips on pages 58 and 59.

MATERIALS

- Craft acrylic paints.
- Triangular makeup sponge and pieces of cardboard, for small stamped design.
- Square block of wood, cardboard, triangular makeup sponge, and wooden spaghetti lifter, for medium stamped design.
- Rectangular block of wood or foam, round bottle cork, cardboard, and rectangular eraser, for large stamped design.

Stamped designs, applied with everyday items like cardboard strips, wooden blocks, and corks, can be used on coordinating pieces like placemats and napkins (right) or on a single bold accessory, such as a toy chest (below).

HOW TO PAINT A SMALL STAMPED DESIGN

1 Apply first paint color to triangular makeup sponge; blot on paper towel. Stamp triangles onto surface, 3" to 4" (7.5 to 10 cm) apart. Allow to dry.

2 Cut a piece of cardboard about 1½" (3.8 cm) long. Apply second paint color to edge of cardboard; blot. Stamp onto surface, varying the direction of the lines and overlapping the triangles; lines may also overlap. Allow to dry.

3 Cut piece of cardboard about 2½" (6.5 cm) long. Apply third paint color to edge; blot and stamp as in step 2.

HOW TO PAINT A MEDIUM STAMPED DESIGN

1 Apply first paint color to wooden block; blot on paper towel. Stamp block prints onto surface, about 2" to 4" (5 to 10 cm) apart. Allow to dry.

2 Fold 5" (12.5 cm) piece of cardboard into triangle, and tape one corner together; sides of triangle do not need to be equal in length. Apply second paint color to the edge of triangle; blot. Stamp onto surface, varying the direction of the triangles and overlapping the block prints. Allow to dry.

3 Apply third paint color to triangular makeup sponge; blot. Stamp triangles onto surface, overlapping previous designs. Allow to dry.

4 Apply fourth paint color to spaghetti lifter; blot. Stamp onto surface, overlapping the previous designs.

HOW TO PAINT A LARGE STAMPED DESIGN

1 Apply first paint color to rectangular block of wood or foam; blot on paper towel. Stamp block prints onto surface, about 4" to 7" (10 to 18 cm) apart, varying the angles. Allow to dry.

2 Fold 12" (30.5 cm) piece of cardboard into triangle as in step 2 for medium stamped design, above. Apply second paint color to edge of triangle; blot. Stamp onto surface, varying the direction of the triangles and overlapping the block prints. Allow to dry.

3 Apply third paint color to round cork; blot. Stamp onto surface, overlapping block prints. Allow to dry.

4 Apply fourth paint color to one long edge of eraser; blot on paper towel, and stamp onto surface, overlapping the block prints. Allow to dry. Stamp with edge of cardboard as in step 2 for the small stamped design, above; stamp randomly in pairs.

EASY FREEHAND DESIGNS

Several simple designs are easy to paint freehand, even if you do not consider yourself an artist. Discover many possible designs by looking at fabrics, wallcoverings, and gift-wrapping papers. When painting repetitive designs, you can allow the designs to vary slightly to emphasize the handmade quality, rather than painstakingly try to paint identical designs. Add interest to the painted pieces by using different designs to highlight separate areas of a single item.

Transfer designs that are more intricate, using the methods on pages 25 to 27. Use appropriate artist's brush to fill in the design areas. When hand painting, you do not have to follow the marked design exactly.

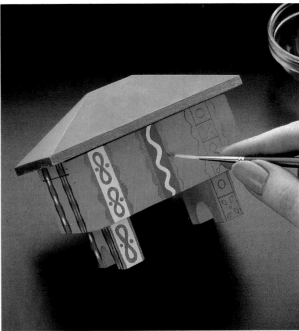

Mark simple freehand designs, using light pencil lines. Fill in the marked areas with paint, allowing the paint to dry between colors.

MORE IDEAS FOR FREEHAND DESIGNS

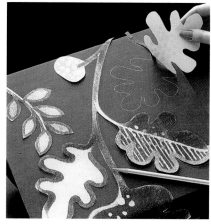

Trace around simple patterns, using a pencil. Fill in the areas with paint; allow to dry. Then add details with contrasting colors.

Mark a grid onto the surface, using a pencil; paint along the lines, using a liner brush. Fill in the areas with a random, light application of paint.

Separate a plain surface into two or more areas; mark the areas with a pencil or with painted lines. Paint each area with a different background color and design.

Paint different designs in each section of the legs of a table or the turned posts of a headboard.

STENCILED DESIGNS

Use stenciled motifs to highlight an area of a room or to simulate architectural details, such as chair rails. A variety of precut stencils is available, with the prices varying widely, usually depending on the intricacy of the design. Or, custom stencils are easily made by tracing designs onto transparent Mylar® sheets. For stencils that coordinate with home furnishings, designs can be adapted from wallpaper, fabric, or artwork. Use a photocopy machine to enlarge or reduce patterns to the desired size.

When stenciling multicolored motifs, it is usually necessary to have a separate stencil for each color. Most precut stencils will have a separate plate for each color and will be numbered according to the sequence for use. A single stencil plate may be used for multiple colors if the spaces between the design areas are large enough to be covered with masking tape. When stenciling multicolored designs, apply the largest part of the design first. When stenciling borders, it is generally best to apply all the repeats of the first color before applying the second color.

Before starting a project, carefully plan the placement of the design. Stencil the design onto paper, and tape it to the surface to check the design placement. Border designs with obvious repeats, such as swags or bows, require careful planning to avoid any partial motifs. If you are stenciling a border, the placement may be influenced by the position of room details, such as windows, doors, and heat vents. It is generally best to start at the most prominent area and work out; the spacing between border repeats may be altered slightly, if necessary.

Use stiff stencil brushes of good quality and sized in proportion to the space being stenciled. Use a separate brush for each color, or clean the brush and allow it to dry before reusing it.

For painting hard surfaces, such as walls and woodwork, use craft acrylic paint mixed with acrylic paint extender, two parts paint to one part extender. This thins the paint and extends the drying time, to allow for more control in shading. You may stencil over a clean, painted surface or over finished wood. If the surface is finished wood, apply a clear finish or sealer to the entire surface after it is stenciled.

For stenciling on fabric, use fabric paints or combine two parts craft acrylic paint to one part textile medium. With either choice of paint, the fabric will not be stiffened. Follow the manufacturer's directions to heat-set the paints. Select fabric that is at least 50 percent cotton, for good penetration of the paint. Avoid fabrics with polished or protective finishes. Prewash fabrics to remove any sizing.

Before beginning the actual project, practice stenciling the designs on paper to become familiar with the way the paint handles and with the shading effects you can achieve.

MATERIALS

GENERAL SUPPLIES

- Precut or custom stencil.
- Craft acrylic paints.
- Acrylic paint extender.
- Stencil brushes.
- Disposable plates.
- Stencil tape.
- Spray adhesive, optional.

FOR CUSTOM STENCILS

- Transparent Mylar sheets.
- Mat knife.
- Cutting surface, such as a self-healing cutting board or cardboard.
- Colored pencils; fine-point permanent-ink marker.

1 Trace design, enlarging or reducing it, if desired (pages 25 to 27). Repeat the design for 13" to 18" (33 to 46 cm) length, making sure the spacing between repeats is consistent.

2 Color the traced design as desired, using colored pencils. Mark placement lines so stencil will be correctly positioned on wall.

3 Position Mylar® sheet over traced design, allowing at least 1" (2.5 cm) border at top and bottom; secure with stencil tape. Trace areas that will be stenciled in first color, using marking pen; transfer placement lines.

4 Trace design areas for each additional color on a separate Mylar sheet. To help align the design, outline areas for previous colors, using dotted lines.

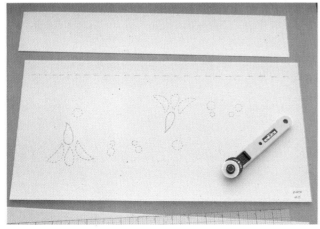

5 Layer Mylar sheets, and check for accuracy. Using mat knife and straightedge, cut outer edges of the stencil plates, leaving 1" to 3" (2.5 to 7.5 cm) border around the design.

6 Cut out marked areas on each sheet, using a mat knife; cut the smallest shapes first, then larger ones. Pull knife toward you as you cut, turning the Mylar sheet, rather than the knife, to change the direction.

HOW TO STENCIL ON WALLS, WOOD & OTHER HARD SURFACES

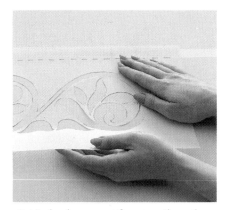

1 Mark placement for stencil on the surface with stencil tape. Position first stencil plate, aligning placement tape with dotted line. Secure the stencil, using stencil tape or spray adhesive.

2 Mix together two parts craft acrylic paint and one part acrylic paint extender on disposable plate.

3 Dip tip of stencil brush into paint mixture. Using a circular motion, blot brush onto folded paper towel until bristles are almost dry.

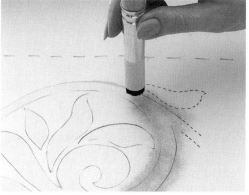

4 Hold brush perpendicular to surface. Blot brush on blank area of stencil plate, using a light circular stroke; if brush strokes are noticeable, blot the brush on a paper towel again, to remove more of the paint.

5 **Circular method**. Hold the brush perpendicular to the surface, and apply paint, using circular motion, within cut areas of stencil. This gives a blended coverage of paint on hard surfaces, such as walls and wood.

5 **Stippling method.** Apply masking tape around bristles, ¼" (6 mm) from the end. Hold the brush perpendicular to surface, and apply paint using up-and-down motion. This gives a textured appearance on hard surfaces; it is also the technique to use for fabrics.

6 Stencil all cut areas of first stencil plate; allow to dry. Remove plate. Secure second plate to surface, matching the design. Apply second color in all cut areas. Repeat for any remaining stencil plates until design is completed.

7 Touch up any glitches or smudges on surface, using background paint and an artist's brush.

HOW TO STENCIL ON FABRICS

1 Prewash fabric to remove any sizing; press fabric. Place fabric, right side up, on medium grit sandpaper, to keep fabric from shifting. Wrap tape around bristles of stencil brush, ¼" (6 mm) from end.

2 Use undiluted fabric paints or mix two parts craft acrylic paint with one part textile medium. Apply paint to the fabric, using stencil brush and stippling method, as on page 47, steps 1 to 7.

3 Heat-set paint when it is thoroughly dry, following the manufacturer's directions for the fabric paint or textile medium that was used; some paints are heat-set from the wrong side of the fabric.

TECHNIQUES FOR SHADED DESIGNS

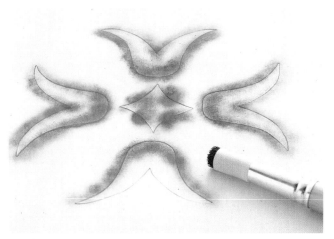

Apply paint within cut areas, leaving centers lighter. For an aged, fade-away effect, use a heavier touch at the base of motif and a lighter touch at the top.

Apply paint, shading the outer edges of cut areas, using a complementary or darker color.

Apply paint to the outer edges within cut areas; allow to dry. Hold a cut piece of Mylar® in place to cover a portion of the area, and apply paint next to edge of the Mylar; for example, cover one half of a leaf, to stencil the veins.

HOW TO CLEAN STENCIL BRUSHES & PLATES

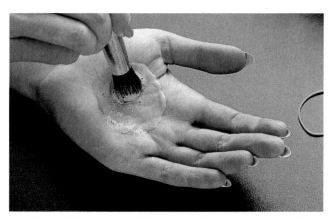

Apply small amount of dishwashing detergent to stencil brush immediately after stenciling is completed. Rub the bristles in palm of your hand in a circular motion, until all paint is removed. Rinse; wrap a rubber band around the bristles, and dry.

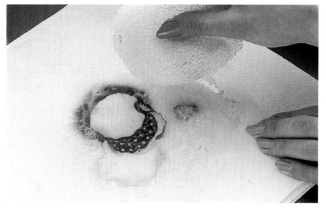

Clean stencil plate on flat surface, using a nylon net scrubbing pad, dishwashing detergent, and warm water. Taking care not to damage the edges of cut openings, rub in circular motion until paint is removed. Rinse and dry.

MORE IDEAS FOR STENCILED DESIGNS

Tray is stenciled with a Southwestern motif of red peppers.

Column and baseboards *are stenciled with coordinating designs for a unified effect.*

Architectural details *are enhanced with the use of stenciled borders.*

Country chair *features coordinating stencil designs on the wooden chair back and fabric seat cushion.*

Fireplace screen *features an elaborate stencil of chestnut leaves.*

DECOUPAGE DESIGNS

Decoupage is the art of decorating surfaces with applied cutouts, then coating them with a translucent finish. It may be used to create elaborate designs on furniture, accessories, and walls.

For intricate ornamentation without a lot of work, make black-and-white photocopies of designs and use them for the cutouts. Then apply a color wash over the cutout, using a paint glaze (page 82) that matches the background. When the decoupage design is completed, the thin layer of paper blends into the surface of the wall or accessory.

To add color or highlighting to the design, you may also apply thinned acrylic paints. This allows you to add color to cutout designs like a bouquet of flowers or a cluster of balloons.

Before applying the cutout, color wash the wall or accessory. Color washing (page 82) provides an especially attractive background and helps the decoupage design blend in softly.

Pictorial design books can inspire designs based on architectural details and eighteenth-century engravings. Or for a light-hearted approach, use advertising art or cartoons.

Color-washed wall *is adorned with decoupage cherubs.*

Wood shelf *is decorated with a decoupage of geometric tribal designs for a primitive look.*

Cabinet (right) features a Flemish still life of fruit and flowers. The decoupage design is highlighted with several accent colors.

HOW TO DECOUPAGE PHOTOCOPIED DESIGNS

MATERIALS

- Low-luster latex enamel paint, for base coat of color-washed wall or accessory.
- Flat latex paint, for color-washing glaze.
- Latex paint conditioner.
- Wallcovering adhesive.

- Sponge applicator.
- Stiff paintbrush and natural-bristle paintbrush.
- Craft acrylic paint in desired colors, for optional highlighting.
- Small, sharp scissors or mat knife.

1 Mix color-washing glaze and color wash the surface of the wall or accessory as on page 82. Allow to dry.

2 Make photocopies of designs, enlarging them to desired size.

3 Cut out the design as desired, using small, sharp scissors or mat knife.

4 Dilute wallcovering adhesive with an equal amount of water; apply an even coat to back side of photocopy cutout, using sponge applicator.

5 Affix photocopy to the surface, smoothing it from the center of the photocopy toward edges, using a dry, stiff paintbrush. Allow to dry.

6 Apply light coat of remaining color-washing glaze to cutout, using natural-bristle paintbrush; blend glaze into color-washed surface. Allow to dry.

7 Add color or highlights to decoupage design, using diluted acrylic paint, if desired; thin the paint as necessary so it is translucent.

*Specialty
Paints &
Glazes*

PAINTING FABRICS

Fabrics can be painted to create unique looks that are coordinated to your decorating scheme. To ensure that the paint will be permanent and to maintain a soft hand in the fabric, use fabric paints. Or use craft acrylic paints with textile medium added; the textile medium allows the paint to penetrate the fibers, for permanent, washable, painted designs. When painting fabrics, avoid a heavy application of paint, to prevent stiffness; in general, the texture of the fabric should show through the paint.

Before painting washable fabrics, remove any sizing from the fabric by laundering it without fabric softener; then press the fabric to remove any wrinkles. To prevent the fabric from shifting during painting, you may tape it to the surface or place it on sandpaper. When painting a completed item, such as a duvet cover or pillow case, place a sheet of plastic under the side you are painting to prevent the paint from penetrating both layers.

After the fabric has been painted, heat-set the paints according to the manufacturer's directions. Usually paint is heat-set by pressing it, using a dry iron and a press cloth. After the paint has been heat-set, use the care method that is recommended for the fabric.

SUGGESTED TECHNIQUES FOR FABRIC PAINTING

The following techniques work well for fabric painting:

Guided designs (page 29);

Swirled designs (page 33);

Stamped designs (page 36);

Stenciled designs (page 44);

Sponge painting (page 78).

Designs and stripes are painted to create the coordinating fabrics shown here. For the fabric on the left, painter's masking tape was used to guide the application of paint in stripes (page 30). For the fabric on the right, geometric shapes cut from masking tape were applied to the fabric, then a texture roller was used for a random application of paint (pages 34 and 35); the centers of the cutout shapes were painted with a small brush.

Hand-painted curtains *combine the techniques for painting stripes (page 30) and sponge painting (page 78).*

HOW TO PAINT ON FABRIC

1 Prewash fabric to remove any sizing, if fabric is washable; press fabric to remove wrinkles.

2 Mix craft acrylic paint with textile medium in ratio recommended by manufacturer; or choose fabric paints that are ready-to-use. Apply the paint to the fabric as desired; allow to dry for 24 hours.

3 Heat-set paints, according to the manufacturer's directions; usually these paints are heat-set by pressing the fabric, using a dry iron and a press cloth.

PAINTING CERAMICS

Glazed ceramics can be hand-painted to coordinate with the decorating scheme of a room. In order to paint on ceramics, it is important that you either prepare the surface by applying a primer recommended for glossy surfaces or that you use the specialty paints designed for ceramic painting. With either method, there is no need to sand the surface to degloss it before painting.

If you use a primer recommended for glossy surfaces, such as a stain-killing primer (page 13), the ceramic piece may be painted using latex or craft acrylic paint; glossy paints are recommended if you want to retain the sheen of glazed ceramic. The paint adheres well to the ceramic, provided the correct primer is used.

For another method of painting ceramics, use one of the ceramic paints that can be applied directly to the glazed ceramic without the use of a primer. These water-based paints, such as Liquitex® Glossies™ and DEKA®-Gloss, are heat-hardened in a low-temperature oven to further improve the ceramic paint's durability, adhesion, and water resistance.

Ceramic paints produce a hand-painted look, often with an uneven coverage that becomes part of the unique character of each piece. They vary in transparency, and some are easier to work with if they are thinned; for maximum durability, dilute the paints with a clear paint medium that is designed for use with ceramic paint. You may also want to spread the paints thinly, allowing the brush strokes to show, to emphasize the hand-painted quality of the design.

Use ceramic paints for display items, such as vases or decorative plates. Although ceramic paints are nontoxic, they are not recommended for use on eating or drinking utensils where food will come into contact with the paint. For best results, hand wash the painted ceramics in lukewarm water with mild detergent.

TWO METHODS FOR PAINTING GLAZED CERAMICS

Primer and latex or craft acrylic paint method. Apply a primer that is recommended for glossy surfaces; allow to dry. Paint over the primer, using latex or craft acrylic paint; any of the painting techniques recommended for latex or craft acrylic paint can be used.

Ceramic paint method. Use ceramic paint, applying it directly to glazed ceramic surface; use desired painting technique, such as stenciling (page 44). Allow to dry. Heat-harden the paint in a low-temperature oven, following the manufacturer's directions.

Faux onyx lamp was painted with a primer recommended for use on glossy surfaces, then painted with a faux onyx finish, using craft acrylic paint as on pages 100 and 101.

Stenciled tiles of this tabletop were painted with ceramic paint. The custom stencil designs were cut and applied as on pages 44 to 47, and the ceramic paints were then heat-hardened before the ceramic tiles were installed.

MORE IDEAS FOR PAINTING CERAMICS

Color-washed ceramic teapot *was painted with a fan brush. To achieve this effect, apply ceramic paint sparingly in cross-hatching brush strokes.*

Swirled designs *(page 33) accent clear glass votives and a coordinating napkin ring. Ceramic paints were used for this technique.*

Glass platter *is accented with translucent ceramic paints. The paints were applied to the underside.*

Old canisters *are given a new look by painting them with a primer suitable for glossy surfaces, then with latex paint. Easy freehand designs (page 40) add a cheerful touch.*

PAINTING WITH GLAZES

Many types of decorative painting require the use of a paint glaze, made by adding paint conditioner (page 10) or paint thickener (page 11) to the paint. With these paint mediums, the drying time of the paint is extended, allowing the additional time needed to manipulate the paint before it sets. The glaze has a creamy texture when wet and forms a translucent top coat once it dries.

Paint glazes were formerly made from oil-based paints mixed with oil glaze. These oil glazes were messy to use, difficult to clean up, and noxious. Water-based latex and acrylic glazes, on the other hand, are easier to use, safer for the user and the environment, and lower in cost.

In this section, the basic glaze (below, right) is used for several types of decorative painting, including strié, combing, rag rolling, texturizing, and, sometimes, sponging. The glaze is varied slightly for color washing (page 82), antiquing (page 84), faux wood grain (page 110), and faux moiré (page 116). Without the use of paint glazes, all of these finishes would be nearly impossible to achieve.

TECHNIQUES FOR PAINTING WITH GLAZE

Strié (page 66) is the striped effect achieved when a natural-bristle paintbrush is dragged through a wet coat of paint glaze.

Combing (page 68) also produces a striped effect when a comb is run through wet glaze. For this technique, you may use one of the combing tools available from craft and art stores, or make a comb by cutting V grooves into a rubber squeegee or a piece of mat board. Use the basic glaze for combing, or, for more distinct lines and a more opaque effect, use a thickened glaze (page 68).

Rag rolling (page 71) creates an allover mottled look. Different effects can be achieved, depending on which method is used. In the "ragging-on" method, a rag is dipped into the paint glaze, wrung out, and rolled in a random pattern across a surface that has a base coat of paint. In the "ragging-off" method, a coat of paint glaze is applied over a base coat; then a rag is rolled through the wet glaze to form patterns.

Texturizing (page 74) uses a number of household items that can be dragged, blotted, stippled, or rolled to create a pattern with glaze. Some possible items include corrugated cardboard, cheesecloth, plastic wrap, and crumpled paper. As with ragging-on and ragging-off, you can either apply the glaze directly to the item and then onto the base-coated surface, or you can move the item through a coat of wet glaze applied over a base coat of paint.

Paint finishes using glaze include combing (orange), rag rolling (green), texturizing (purple), and strié (gold).

TIPS FOR USING PAINT GLAZE

Use a paint roller to apply the glaze when even coverage is desired or when painting a large surface, such as a wall.

Use a paintbrush to apply the glaze when a paint finish with more variation and pattern in the surface is desired or when painting a small item.

Use a sponge applicator to apply the glaze when smooth coverage is desired or when painting a small item.

Manipulate the glaze while it is still wet. Although humidity affects the setting time, the glaze can usually be manipulated for a few minutes.

Work with an assistant when using glaze on a large surface. While one person applies the glaze, the other can manipulate it.

Protect the surrounding area with a drop cloth or plastic sheet and wear old clothing, because working with glaze can be messy.

Use wide painter's tape (page 14) to mask off the surrounding surfaces. Firmly rub the edges of the tape, to ensure that the glaze will not seep under it.

BASIC GLAZE

Mix together the following ingredients:

One part latex or craft acrylic paint in desired sheen;

One part latex paint conditioner, such as Floetrol®;

One part water.

STRIÉ

Strié is a series of irregular streaks in a linear pattern, created by using a paint glaze. Especially suitable for walls, this painting technique can also be used for furniture pieces with flat surfaces.

For this technique, use the basic glaze and instructions on page 65. To achieve the strié effect, pull a dry, wide natural-bristle paintbrush through the glaze while it is wet. Before the glaze completely sets, the lines can be softened by lightly dry-brushing the surface with a soft natural-bristle paintbrush.

For large surfaces, it is helpful to work with an assistant. After one person has applied the glaze, the other person brushes through the glaze before it dries, to achieve the strié effect. If you are working alone, limit yourself to smaller sections, if possible, since the glaze must be wet to create this look. If it is necessary to interrupt the process, stop only when a section is completed.

Because it can be messy to apply a strié finish, wear old clothing and protect the surrounding area with drop cloths and wide painter's tape. Firmly rub the edges of the tape, to ensure that the glaze will not seep under it.

Strié lends itself well to tone-on-tone colorations, such as ivory over white or tones of blue, although the color selection is not limited to this look. To become familiar with the technique and test the colors, first apply the finish to a sheet of cardboard, such as mat board.

HOW TO APPLY A STRIÉ PAINT FINISH

MATERIALS

- Low-luster latex enamel in desired color, for the base coat.
- Latex paint in desired sheen and color, for the glaze.
- Latex paint conditioner, such as Floetrol®.
- Wide natural-bristle brush.
- Soft natural-bristle paintbrush.

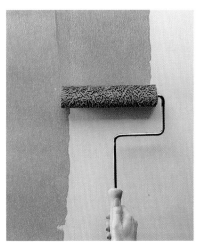

1 Prepare surface (page 16). Apply base coat of low-luster latex enamel; allow to dry. Mix glaze (page 65); apply over base coat in a vertical section about 18" (46 cm) wide, using paint roller or natural-bristle paintbrush.

2 Drag a dry, wide natural-bristle paintbrush through wet glaze, immediately after glaze is applied; work from top to bottom in full, continuous brush strokes. To keep brush rigid, hold bristles of brush against surface with handle tilted slightly toward you. Repeat until desired effect is achieved.

3 Wipe the paintbrush occasionally on clean, dry rag to remove excess glaze, for a uniform strié look. Or rinse brush in clear water, and wipe dry.

4 Brush surface lightly after glaze has dried for about 5 minutes, if softer lines are desired; use soft natural-bristle brush, and keep brush strokes in same direction as streaks.

COMBING

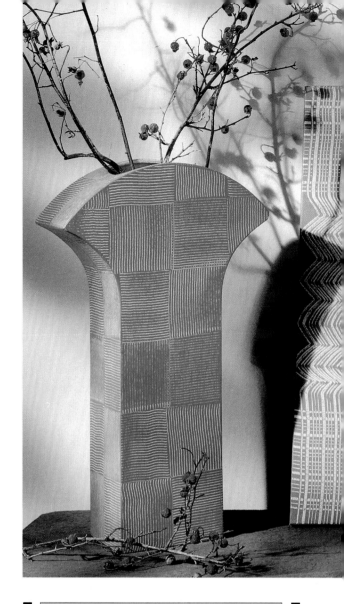

Combing is a decorative painting technique that has been used for many years, as is evident by the number of antiques with this finish. For this technique, a paint glaze is applied over a base coat of paint. Narrow lines or stripes in the finish are created as you drag the teeth of a comb through the paint glaze, removing some of the glaze to reveal the base coat of paint. For a pronounced effect, the color of the paint glaze may contrast with that of the base coat.

The rubber combing tools available at craft and art stores work well for this paint finish. Metal combs are also available, but their rigid teeth may scratch the base coat. If desired, you can make your own comb by cutting V grooves into a rubber squeegee or a piece of mat board.

A variety of combed patterns, such as wavy lines, scallops, crisscrosses, zigzags, and basket weaves, can be created. If you are unsatisfied with a particular pattern, the glaze can be wiped off while it is still wet, then reapplied; or the wet glaze can be smoothed out with a paintbrush, then combed into a different pattern.

You may use either the basic glaze of paint, water, and paint conditioner or a thickened glaze of paint and paint thickener. The basic glaze produces a more translucent look and works well on walls and other surfaces without adding texture to the surface. The thickened glaze gives an opaque look with more distinct lines and texture; some thickeners may cause bubbles in the paint mixture, but these bubbles can be brushed out as the glaze is applied.

In order to comb the glaze while it is still wet, apply it to a small area at a time. It is important to wipe off the combing tool after each pass, to prevent buildup on the comb. For more information on working with glaze, see page 65.

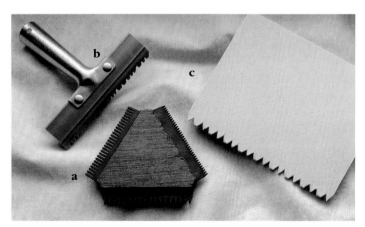

Combing tools, such as a rubber comb **(a),** may be purchased. Or make your own combs by using a pair of shears or an artist's knife to cut V grooves in a rubber squeegee **(b)** or mat board **(c).**

BASIC GLAZE

Mix together the following ingredients:

One part latex or craft acrylic paint in desired sheen;

One part latex paint conditioner;

One part water.

THICKENED GLAZE

Mix together the following ingredients:

Two parts latex or craft acrylic paint in desired sheen;

One part acrylic paint thickener (although thickeners are developed for use with acrylic paints, they can also be used with latex paint).

HOW TO APPLY A COMBED PAINT FINISH

MATERIALS

- Low-luster latex enamel paint in desired color, for base coat.
- Latex paint or craft acrylic paint in desired sheen and color, for glaze.
- Latex paint conditioner, for basic glaze; or acrylic paint thickener, for thickened glaze.
- Paintbrush, paint roller, or sponge applicator.
- Combing tool, opposite.
- Clear finish or aerosol clear acrylic sealer, optional.

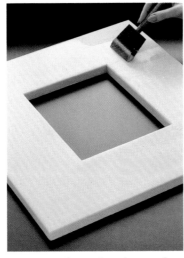

1 Prepare the surface (page 16). Apply base coat of low-luster latex enamel to surface, using a sponge applicator, paintbrush, or paint roller. Allow to dry.

2 Mix basic or thickened glaze (opposite); apply to small area at a time, using a sponge applicator, paintbrush, or paint roller. Drag combing tool through wet glaze to create pattern. Allow to dry. Apply clear finish or sealer, if desired.

RAG ROLLING

Rag rolling is a painting technique that gives a rich, textural look with an allover mottled effect. It works well for walls and other flat surfaces, such as dresser tops and drawers, shelves, bookends, and doors. The basic paint glaze on page 65 can be used in either of the two techniques for rag rolling, *ragging-on* and *ragging-off*.

In ragging-on, a rag is saturated in the prepared paint glaze, wrung out, rolled up, and then rolled across a surface that has been base-coated with low-luster latex enamel paint. Rag-on a single application of glaze over the base coat, for a bold pattern. Or, for a more subtle, blended look, rag-on two or more applications of glaze.

In ragging-off, apply a coat of paint glaze over the base coat, using a paintbrush or paint roller; then roll up a rag and roll it over the wet glaze to remove some of the glaze. This process may be repeated for more blending, but you must work fast, because the glaze dries quickly.

If you are using the ragging-off method on large surfaces, such as walls, it is helpful to have an assistant. After one person applies the glaze, the second person can rag-off the area before the glaze dries. While it is not necessary to complete the entire room in one session, it is important that you complete an entire wall.

With either method, test the technique and the colors that you intend to use on a large piece of cardboard, such as mat board, before you start the project. Generally, a lighter color is used for the base coat, with a darker color for the glaze.

Feel free to experiment with the technique as you test it, perhaps rag rolling two different glaze colors over the base coat. Or try taping off an area, such as a border strip, and rag rolling a second or third color within the taped area.

Because the glaze can be messy to work with, apply a wide painter's tape around the area to be painted and use drop cloths to protect the surrounding surfaces. Wear old clothes and rubber gloves, and keep an old towel nearby to wipe your hands after you wring out the rags.

MATERIALS

- Low-luster latex enamel paint, for base coat.
- Latex or craft acrylic paint and latex paint conditioner, for glaze; 1 qt. (0.9 L) of each is sufficient for the walls of 12 ft. × 14 ft. (3.7 × 4.33 m) room.
- Paint pail; rubber gloves; old towel; lint-free rags, about 24" (61 cm) square.

Rag rolling *adds textural interest to walls, furniture, and accessories. Opposite, ragging-on was used for the walls, while ragging-off was used for the vase. The tabletop above was painted by ragging-off.*

HOW TO APPLY A RAG-ROLLED PAINT FINISH
USING THE RAGGING-ON METHOD

1 Prepare surface (page 16). Apply a base coat of low-luster latex enamel, using paintbrush or paint roller. Allow to dry.

2 Mix basic glaze (page 65) in pail. Dip lint-free rag into glaze, saturating entire rag; wring out well. Wipe excess glaze from hands with old towel.

3 Roll up the rag irregularly; then fold in half to a width equal to both hands.

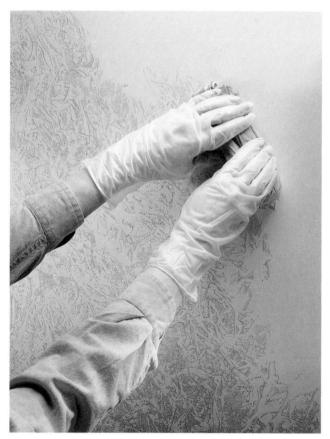

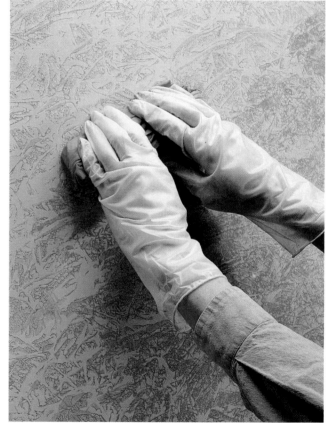

4 Roll the rag over surface, working upward at varying angles. Rewet rag whenever necessary, and wring out.

5 Repeat the application, if more coverage is desired.

HOW TO APPLY A RAG-ROLLED PAINT FINISH
USING THE RAGGING-OFF METHOD

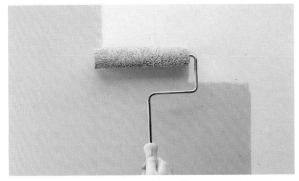

1 Apply base coat of low-luster latex enamel, using paintbrush or paint roller. Allow to dry.

2 Mix basic glaze (page 65); pour into a paint tray. Apply the glaze over the base coat, using paint roller or paint pad.

3 Roll up lint-free rag irregularly; fold in half to width of both hands. Roll the rag through the wet glaze, working upward at varying angles.

COLOR EFFECTS

As shown in the examples below, the color of the base coat is not affected when the ragging-on method is used. With the ragging-off method, the color of the base coat is changed, because the glaze is applied over the entire surface, and then some glaze is removed with a rag to soften the background.

Ragging-on is used, applying aqua glaze over a white base coat. The white base coat remains unchanged.

Ragging-off is used, applying aqua glaze over a white base coat. The white base coat is covered with the glaze, then appears as a lighter aqua background when some of the glaze is removed.

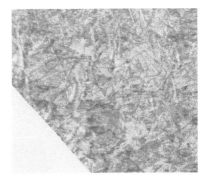

Ragging-on and ragging-off are both used. First a taupe glaze is ragged-on over a white base coat. Then a rust glaze is ragged-off, changing the white base coat to a lighter shade of rust.

TEXTURIZING

There are several ways to achieve a finish that has visual texture with paint glaze in addition to the methods for strié, combing, and rag rolling, using any number of household items and painting supplies. Rolled or bent pieces of corrugated cardboard, cheesecloth, crumpled paper, raffia, plastic wrap, carved potatoes, and scrub brushes create interesting textured effects. The list of items is as endless as your imagination.

For these finishes, use the basic glaze and instructions on page 65. You may apply a coat of glaze directly to the surface, then manipulate it or partially remove it by dabbing the glaze with the item or items you have selected. Or using the alternate method, the glaze may be applied to the selected items, then printed onto the surface. To become familiar with the methods and determine which effects you prefer, experiment with both methods, using a variety of items.

Apply a base coat of paint, using a good-quality low-luster latex enamel, before you apply the glaze. The base coat and the glaze may be in contrasting colors, such as emerald green over white. For a more subtle look, try a tone-on-tone effect, such as two shades of blue, or choose colors that are similar in intensity, such as deep red over deep purple. For even more possibilities, the process can be repeated, using one or more additional colors of glaze. This adds even more visual interest and is especially suitable for small accessories.

MATERIALS

- Low-luster latex enamel paint in desired color, for base coat.
- Latex paint in desired sheen and color, for glaze.
- Latex paint conditioner, such as Floetrol®.
- Items selected for creating the textural effect.

Accessories *(above) have a variety of textural effects, created using folded cheesecloth for the vase, rolled corrugated cardboard for the bowl, and single-face corrugated cardboard for the tray.*

Folding screen *(opposite) features three texturizing methods. For the background, plastic wrap was used to remove some of the glaze. For the border insert at the top, a fan brush was used to apply glaze. For the center inserts, crumpled paper was used to apply glaze.*

HOW TO APPLY A TEXTURIZED PAINT FINISH

1 Prepare surface (page 16). Apply a base coat of low-luster latex enamel, using sponge applicator, paintbrush, or paint roller. Allow to dry.

2 Mix glaze (page 65). Apply glaze to a small area at a time, using sponge applicator, paintbrush, or paint roller. A heavier coat of glaze gives a more opaque finish, and a light coat, a more translucent finish.

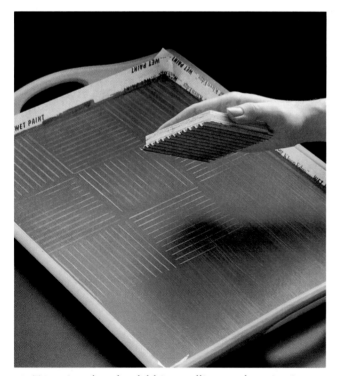

3 Texturize glaze by dabbing, rolling, or dragging items in the glaze to create patterns; rotate item, if desired, to vary the look. Replace the item as necessary, or wipe the excess glaze from item occasionally.

Alternate method. Follow step 1, above. Then apply glaze to selected item, using a sponge applicator, paintbrush, or paint roller; blot on paper towel or cardboard. Dab, roll, or drag glaze-covered item over base coat, to apply glaze to surface randomly or in desired pattern.

Rolled corrugated cardboard is secured by taping it together. Use corrugated end to make designs in coat of wet glaze (left). Or apply glaze directly to cardboard; blot, and print designs on surface (right).

Single-face corrugated cardboard is cut to the desired shape. To make designs, press corrugated side in coat of wet glaze (left). Or apply glaze directly to corrugated side; blot, and print designs on surface (right).

Cheesecloth is folded into a flat pad and pressed into coat of wet glaze (left). Or apply glaze directly to a folded flat pad of cheesecloth, then imprint the cheesecloth onto the surface (right).

Plastic wrap is wrinkled slightly and placed over coat of wet glaze; press lightly, and peel off (left). Or apply glaze directly to plastic wrap. Then place plastic wrap on the surface, folding and crinkling it; peel off (right).

Crumpled paper is pressed into coat of wet glaze (left). Or apply glaze directly to paper; press onto the surface, crumpling the paper (right).

Fan brush is pressed into wet glaze, making uniform rows of fan-shaped impressions (left). Or apply glaze directly to fan brush, and print fan-shaped designs on surface (right).

SPONGE PAINTING

Sponge painting produces a soft, mottled effect and is one of the easiest techniques to use. To achieve this paint finish, use a natural sea sponge to dab paint onto a surface. Cellulose or synthetic sponges should not be used, because they tend to leave identical impressions with hard, defined edges.

The sponged look can be varied, depending on the number of paint colors applied, the sequence in which you apply the colors, and the distance between the sponge impressions. You can use semigloss, low-luster, or flat latex paint for the base coat and the sponging. Or for a translucent finish, use a paint glaze that consists of paint, paint conditioner, and water; make the glaze as on page 65.

To create stripes, borders, or panels, use painter's masking tape to mask off the desired areas of the surface after the first color of sponged paint is applied. Then apply another color to the unmasked areas.

MATERIALS

- Craft acrylic or latex paints in desired sheens and colors, for base coat and for sponging.
- Natural sea sponge.
- Painter's masking tape.
- Carpenter's level, for painting stripes, borders, or panels.

Napkin *has been sponge painted, using fabric paints instead of latex or craft acrylic paints. Refer to the tips for using fabric paints on pages 58 and 59. For sponge painting on fabrics, do not blend the colors with a wet sponge.*

Urn and wall *(opposite) show two different applications for sponge painting. The urn is sponged following its swirled design lines; for sheen, gold metallic paint was applied last. The wall is sponge painted in stripes as on page 81.*

HOW TO SPONGE PAINT

1 Prepare surface (page 16). Apply base coat of desired color. Allow to dry. Rinse sea sponge in water to soften it; squeeze out most of the water. Saturate sponge with paint or with paint glaze (page 65). Blot the sponge lightly on paper towel.

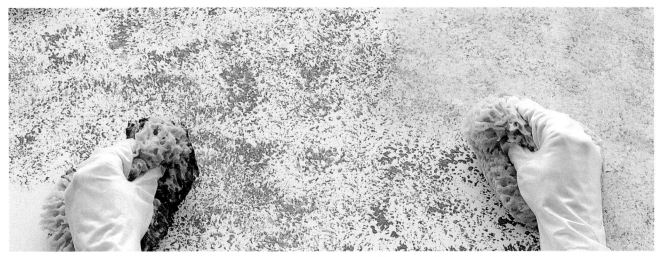

2 Press sponge repeatedly onto surface, as shown at left; work quickly in small areas, and change position of sponge often. Blot paint on surface immediately, using wet sea sponge in other hand, as shown at right; this causes the paint to bleed, for a softened, blended look. Some of the paint is removed with the wet sponge.

3 Continue to apply the first paint color to entire project, blotting with moist sponge. Repeat steps with one or more additional colors of paint, if desired. Allow paint to dry between colors.

4 **Optional feathering.** Apply final color of paint, using a light, sweeping motion instead of dabbing.

HOW TO SPONGE PAINT STRIPES, BORDERS, OR PANELS

1 Follow steps 1 to 3, opposite. Allow paint to dry thoroughly. Mark light plumb line, using a pencil and carpenter's level. Position first row of painter's masking tape along this line.

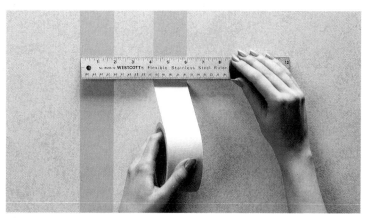

2 Measure and position remaining rows of painter's masking tape to mark stripes, borders, or panel areas.

3 Apply second paint color to the unmasked areas of the surface. Allow paint to dry.

4 Remove the painter's masking tape, revealing two variations of sponge painting.

COLOR EFFECTS

When related colors are used for sponge painting, such as two warm colors or two cool colors, a harmonious look is achieved. For a bolder and more unexpected look, sponge paint in a combination of warm and cool colors.

Warm colors like yellow and orange blend together for an exciting effect.

Cool colors like green and blue blend together for a tranquil effect.

Warm and cool colors like yellow and blue combine boldly, but sponge painting softens the effect.

COLOR WASHING

Color washing is an easy paint finish that gives walls a translucent, watercolored look. It adds visual texture to flat drywall surfaces, and it further emphasizes the already textured surface of a plaster or stucco wall.

In this technique, a color-washing glaze is applied in a cross-hatching fashion over a base coat of low-luster latex enamel, using a natural-bristle paintbrush. As the glaze begins to dry, it can be softened further by brushing the surface with a dry natural-bristle paintbrush. Complete one wall before moving on to the next or before stopping. Store any remaining glaze in a reclosable container between painting sessions.

The color-washing glaze can be either lighter or darker than the base coat. For best results, use two colors that are closely related or consider using a neutral color like beige or white for either the base coat or the glaze. Because the glaze is messy to work with, cover the floor and furniture with drop cloths and apply painter's tape along the ceiling and moldings.

COLOR-WASHING GLAZE

Mix together the following ingredients:

One part flat latex paint;

One part latex paint conditioner;

Two parts water.

HOW TO COLOR WASH WALLS

MATERIALS

- Low-luster latex enamel paint, for base coat.
- Flat latex paint, for color-washing glaze.
- Latex paint conditioner, for color-washing glaze.
- Paint roller.
- Two 3" to 4" (7.5 to 10 cm) natural-bristle paintbrushes for each person.
- Drop cloths; painter's tape.

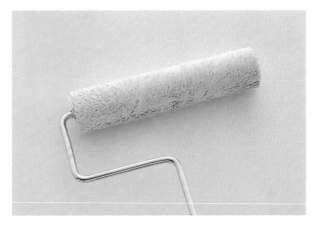

1 Prepare surface (page 16). Apply base coat of low-luster latex enamel paint in the desired color, using paint roller. Allow to dry.

2 Mix the color-washing glaze, opposite. Dip paintbrush into the glaze; remove excess glaze against rim of the container. Apply the glaze to wall in crosshatching manner, beginning in one corner. The more you brush over the surface, the softer the appearance.

3 Brush over the surface, if desired, using a dry natural-bristle paintbrush, to soften the look. Wipe excess glaze from the brush as necessary.

COLOR EFFECTS

Select colors for the base coat and the glaze that are closely related, or use at least one neutral color. A darker glaze over a lighter base coat gives a mottled effect. A lighter glaze over a darker base coat gives a chalky or watercolored effect.

Apply darker top coat, such as a medium turquoise, over lighter base coat, such as white.

Apply a lighter top coat, such as white, over a darker base coat, such as coral.

Apply two shades of a color, such as a medium blue top coat over a light blue base coat.

ANTIQUING

Country-style hutch was stenciled (page 44), then given an antiqued finish (opposite).

Collection of ceramic pots has been painted in a variety of colors, then antiqued.

This antiqued finish gives accessories and furniture a timeworn look. To achieve this effect, an earth-tone glaze is rubbed on over a base coat of paint that has been sealed with an acrylic sealer. For more country charm, the item can be stenciled before the paint is sealed and antiqued.

This technique calls for a special antiquing glaze made by combining acrylic paint thickener with acrylic paints. After the glaze is applied, some of it is removed for a worn look, leaving glaze in the corners and crevices. Leave most of the glaze on the item for a heavily antiqued look, or remove most of it for a minimal effect.

HOW TO APPLY AN ANTIQUED PAINT FINISH

MATERIALS

- Flat latex paint, for base coat.
- Synthetic-bristle paintbrush.
- Acrylic paint thickener.
- Burnt umber craft acrylic paint.
- Burnt sienna craft acrylic paint.
- Aerosol clear acrylic sealer in gloss finish.

ANTIQUING GLAZE

Mix together the following ingredients:

One part burnt umber acrylic paint;

One part burnt sienna acrylic paint;

Two parts acrylic paint thickener.

1 Prepare surface (page 16). Apply a base coat of flat latex paint, using synthetic brush. Paint stenciled designs or other decorative effects after the base coat is dry. Apply several light coats of aerosol clear acrylic sealer in gloss finish. Allow to dry.

2 Mix antiquing glaze, above. Apply the glaze over base coat to a small area at a time, using a sponge applicator or paintbrush.

3 Wipe surface to remove some of the antiquing glaze, using clean lint-free rag; leave a heavier amount of glaze at edges, corners, and crevices. For more control, rub lightly to remove a small amount of the glaze at a time. Rub in one direction for the look of antiqued wood; rub in circular motion for random effect. Allow to dry. Apply several light coats of aerosol clear acrylic sealer.

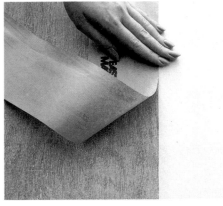

For large surfaces. Prepare entire surface as in step 1, above. To divide area, apply painter's tape in direction of strokes; apply glaze to one side of tape as in steps 2 and 3. Remove the tape; apply new tape, aligning the edge with glaze, as shown. Apply glaze to other side. Apply sealer.

Faux Finishes

FAUX GRANITE

To duplicate the look of natural granite is very easy. By combining the techniques of sponge painting and specking, you can create a simulated granite that is so realistic that people may actually have to touch it before they realize it is a faux finish.

Natural granite is formed from molten stone and has a crystalline appearance. Granite colors from different regions of the world vary greatly, depending on how fast the molten lava cooled. The most common types of granite in America are composed of earth tones in burnt umber, raw umber, warm gray, black, and white. Some exotic granites consist of a rich combination of burgundy, purple, black, and gray; a fiery mix of copper, umber, black, and gray; the cool opalescence of metallic blue, black, pearl, and gray; and a warm combination of orange, red, and salmon. The color combinations for the granites shown here are given on page 91.

Since this is painted granite, the color combinations need not be realistic. You can use this technique in any color combination, to suit a particular decorating scheme.

Metal lamp and wooden frame *are finished in two coordinating colors of granite.*

Molded plastic boxes, *inexpensive to purchase, are transformed into rich-looking accessories.*

Plaster pedestal, *finished in faux granite, becomes the base for a glass-top table.*

HOW TO APPLY A FAUX GRANITE PAINT FINISH

MATERIALS

- Flat latex or craft acrylic paint, for base coat.
- Flat latex or craft acrylic paint in desired colors, for sponging and specking; metallic paint may be used for one of the colors.
- Natural sea sponge.
- Fine-bristle scrub brush or toothbrush.
- Low-luster aerosol clear acrylic sealer or clear finish.

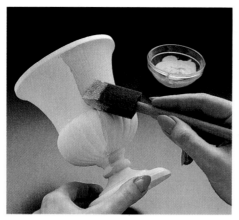

1 Prepare surface (page 16). Apply a base coat of flat latex or craft acrylic paint in white, gray, or black.

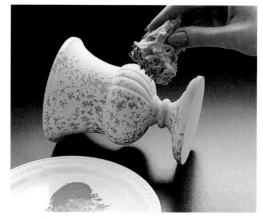

2 Dilute one paint color for sponging, one part paint to one part water, or to the consistency of ink; it may not be necessary to dilute metallic paint. Apply paint to surface in an up-and-down motion, using sea sponge.

3 Blot paint evenly with a clean, dampened sea sponge, immediately after applying it. This mottles the paint, blends it slightly with background color, and increases transparency. If the effect is not pleasing, wipe it off with a damp cloth before it dries.

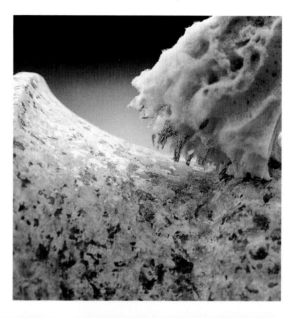

4 Repeat steps 2 and 3 for remaining colors of paint for sponging, allowing each color to dry before the next color is applied. Allow some of the base coat to show through the other layers, to create depth.

5 Apply diluted white, gray, or black paint to surface, using the specking technique, opposite. Speck the surface evenly in a light or moderate application.

6 Apply a low-luster aerosol clear acrylic sealer or clear finish to add sheen and depth and increase durability.

HOW TO ADD SPECKING

1 Dilute the paint for specking with water as in step 2, opposite. Test the paint consistency and technique by specking on cardboard before specking the actual project. Dip the bristles of a fine-bristle scrub brush or a toothbrush into the paint mixture. Dab once on a dry paper towel, to remove excess moisture and prevent drips.

2 Hold the brush next to surface; run craft stick or finger along bristles, causing specks of paint to spatter onto surface. Experiment with how fast you move the craft stick and how far away you hold the brush. Too much paint on the brush may cause paint to drip or run.

COLOR EFFECTS

Granite colors vary from one part of the world to another. Use the color combinations below to simulate some of the natural granites that exist.

Apply a black base coat. Use sea sponge to apply paints in medium gray, light gray, and metallic silver. Speck with more light gray paint.

Apply a dark ivory base coat. Use a sea sponge to apply paints in brown, medium gray, dark gray, and black. Speck with more black paint.

Apply a medium gray base coat. Use sea sponge to apply dark gray, black, and metallic copper. Speck with more black paint.

FAUX MOSAIC

Simulate a mosaic design with a painting technique that uses small pieces of sponge as stamps. For easier handling, several pieces of sponge are glued to a small piece of foam board, allowing you to create intricate stamped designs in a single printing. Make a separate stamp for each mosaic design and each color, because the stamps cannot be cleaned. If the project is not finished in one day, used stamps may be kept overnight in tightly sealed plastic bags.

Faux mosaic works for smooth or textured surfaces. Use it to create a border design along the ceiling, to frame a window or archway, or to embellish the wall below a chair rail. Or use faux mosaic on accessories like vases and planter stands.

Before you start painting, you may want to sketch the mosaic design to scale on graph paper as shown on page 94.

MATERIALS

- Flat or low-luster latex or craft acrylic paint, for base coat.
- Latex or craft acrylic paints in desired colors, for mosaic design.
- Cellulose sponge; slightly dampened sponges are easier to use.
- Pieces of foam board; craft glue; disposable plates; artist's eraser.
- Utility knife or razor blade; ruler.
- Carpenter's level, for marking walls.
- Transparent Mylar® sheets and painter's masking tape, for mosaic design motifs.

Walls showcase faux mosaic designs. Above, the border design is created entirely from rows of squares. Opposite, the intricate design includes several custom-designed motifs.

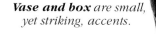

Vase and box are small, yet striking, accents.

HOW TO MAKE THE STAMPS FOR A MOSAIC DESIGN

1 Cut cellulose sponge into ¾" (2 cm) squares or other mosaic shapes, using utility knife.

2 Cut piece of foam board with a utility knife, to be used as a base for stamp. For an overall grid design, cut 2" × 2" (5 × 5 cm) base to hold four ¾" (2 cm) sponge squares. For a straight-line design, cut 1" × 4" (2.5 × 10 cm) base to hold four sponges. For small details, cut a 1" × 1" (2.5 × 2.5 cm) base to hold one sponge.

3 Glue sponges of same height to base, spacing them about ⅛" (3 mm) apart. To keep mosaic design irregular in appearance, do not space sponges precisely. Allow glue to dry.

4 Make stamps for mosaic motifs by cutting desired shape from foam board, for base. Cut sponges into desired shapes to fill design area; glue pieces to base, spacing them about ⅛" (3 mm) apart. Allow glue to dry.

HOW TO PAINT A FAUX MOSAIC DESIGN

1 Measure area to be painted with mosaic design. Make diagram of the area on graph paper, drawing the mosaic design to scale on the diagram, using pencil; include any details, such as motifs or borders.

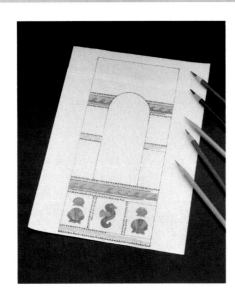

2 Apply base coat in the desired color; use the color-washing technique, if desired (page 82). Use a mortar color for base coat, for the look of real grout. Allow to dry.

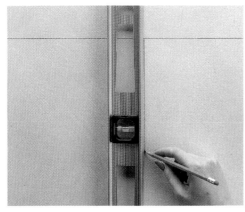

3 Mark outer guidelines of the design area lightly on base-coated surface, using a pencil; to mark walls, use carpenter's level. Mark any other significant placement lines, such as dividing lines, borders, and motifs.

4 Pour small amount of latex or craft acrylic paint in each color for mosaic stamps onto disposable plates. Dip stamp lightly into paint for a one-color stamp **(a).** Or apply paint colors to individual pieces of sponge **(b).** Blot onto paper to remove excess paint.

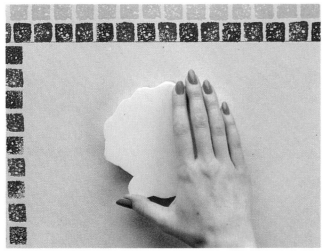

5 Stamp mosaic design onto surface, using marked lines as a guide, stamping any dividing lines, borders, and motifs; reapply paint to stamp as necessary. Use separate stamp for each mosaic design and color combination.

6 Cut Mylar® for each motif, ⅛" (3 mm) larger on all sides. Secure folded painter's masking tape to back of Mylar. Mask off stamped motifs by securing Mylar to the surface over the motif.

7 Finish stamping background area. When stamping the area surrounding motifs, allow the stamps to overlap the Mylar. Allow paint to dry.

8 Remove the Mylar from motif areas. Erase any marked lines that are not covered with paint, using artist's eraser.

MARBLED FAUX FINISHES

Several types of minerals, including serpentine, onyx, alabaster, and breccia, have a marbled or veined appearance and exist in nature in a wide variety of colors. These looks can be duplicated in paint finishes, using a technique called *veining* combined with other techniques.

For the veining, acrylic extender and acrylic thickener are used alongside the paint to create veins that fluctuate from opaque to translucent. A feather is used in an irregular, trembling motion to apply the veins.

Faux onyx *(below) resembles the black-and-white onyx rock that is related to marble. Banded areas of chalky white are overlayed on a black background and outlined with white veins.*

Faux alabaster *has the white, translucent appearance of alabaster, often used for carved vases and ornaments. To achieve alabaster's subtle effect, a base coat of white low-luster enamel is veined with soft gray craft acrylic paint. The entire surface is then whitewashed with diluted paint and softly dry-brushed.*

Faux breccia *has the irregular, random appearance of real breccia, which is composed of various fragmented rocks, sometimes including marble. Although the painting technique is similar to that of faux alabaster, faux breccia has a bolder look, with areas of peach outlined in gray veining to contrast with the white background. For a more* *fragmented look, specks of gray are scattered lightly over the surface. On accessories, the veining can be closely spaced and several peach areas can be applied. When using faux breccia on large surfaces like walls, use less veining and space the peach areas farther apart.*

Faux serpentine *has the variegated dark-green color of the mineral serpentine, as well as its mottled appearance and veins of white. This look is achieved by applying a blend of greens with a sponge in an up-and-down stippling motion, then adding the veins with a feather.*

HOW TO APPLY A FAUX SERPENTINE PAINT FINISH

MATERIALS

- Black craft acrylic or flat latex paint, for base coat.
- Craft acrylic paints in dark hunter green, medium green, light blue-green, and white; purchase craft acrylic paints in squeeze bottles for easier application.
- Acrylic paint thickener.
- Acrylic paint extender.

- Sponge applicator or synthetic-bristle paintbrush.
- Natural sea sponge.
- Turkey or pheasant feather.
- Disposable plates.
- High-gloss aerosol clear acrylic sealer.

1 Prepare surface (page 16). Apply base coat of black acrylic or flat latex paint. Allow to dry.

2 Squeeze dark hunter green, medium green, and light blue-green paints in random spiraling lines onto disposable plate, overlapping the paint colors.

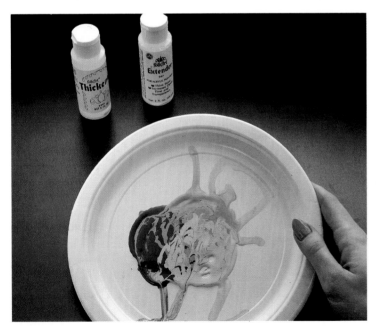

3 Squeeze spiraling lines of thickener and extender over green paints. Tilt plate so colors mingle and marbleize.

4 Dip dampened sea sponge into marbleized green paint; blot lightly onto paper towel to remove excess paint.

5 Dab sponge lightly and repeatedly onto black base coat in an up-and-down stippling motion, turning sponge for random pattern. Allow some base coat to show, and do not mix paint colors together completely; the thickener and extender help keep the colors separate. Allow to dry.

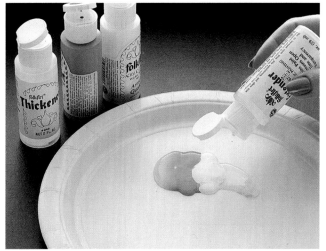

6 Apply long pools of white and medium green paint onto another disposable plate. Apply pool of thickener on one side of paints and extender on the other.

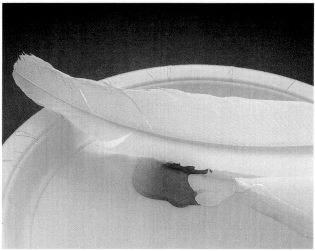

7 Run edge of feather through pools, picking up some thickener, paints, and extender on feather.

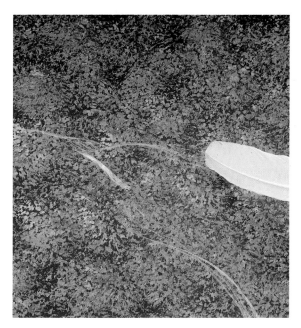

8 Place tip of feather onto surface; drag feather along, fidgeting and turning it slightly in your hand to create veins. Apply veins in diagonal direction, crisscrossing them as desired. The thickener and extender vary the veins so some areas are opaque and some are translucent.

9 Allow paint to dry. Apply several light coats of high-gloss aerosol acrylic sealer.

HOW TO APPLY A FAUX ONYX PAINT FINISH

MATERIALS

- Black craft acrylic or flat latex paint, for base coat.
- White craft acrylic paint.
- Acrylic paint thickener.
- Acrylic paint extender.

- Natural sea sponge.
- Two turkey or pheasant feathers.
- Disposable plate.
- High-gloss aerosol clear acrylic sealer.

1 Prepare surface (page 16). Apply a base coat of black craft acrylic or flat latex paint. Allow to dry.

2 Apply a long pool of white paint onto a disposable plate. Apply pool of thickener on one side of white paint and extender on the other.

3 Run edge of feather through pools, picking up some thickener, paint, and extender on feather; cover the entire length of feather. Blot excess onto paper towel.

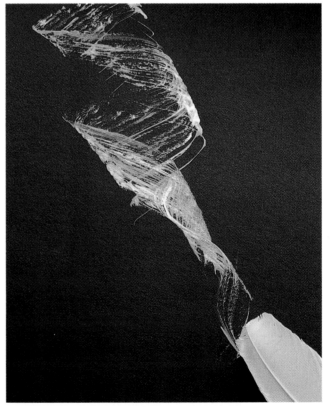

4 Zigzag the feather across base coat in 3" to 4" (7.5 to 10 cm) irregular diagonal bands, with some of the bands meeting or intersecting. Work on only two or three bands at a time, because paint dries quickly.

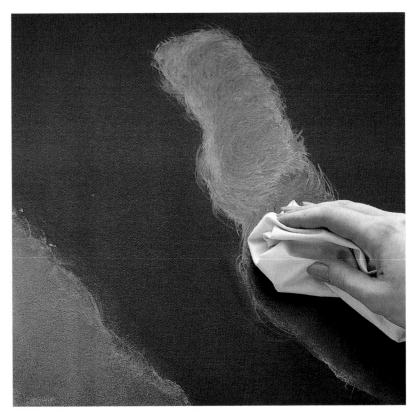

5 Smear the bands of white in a circular motion, using moist sea sponge, for the look of softened light clouds.

6 Rub the bands lightly while still wet, using a dry rag, to give them the appearance of dust on a chalkboard; do not rub over the black base coat. Reapply white paint if too much is rubbed away. If surface dries too quickly, apply water, then rub with rag to soften. Allow to dry.

7 Run edge of the feather through pools of thickener, paint, and extender; blot on paper towel. Place tip of feather onto surface; drag the feather along, fidgeting it and turning it slightly in your hand to create veins. Outline chalky bands with veins; apply more veins in a diagonal direction, crisscrossing them as desired. The thickener and extender vary the veins so some areas are opaque and some are translucent. Allow paint to dry. Apply several coats of high-gloss aerosol clear acrylic sealer.

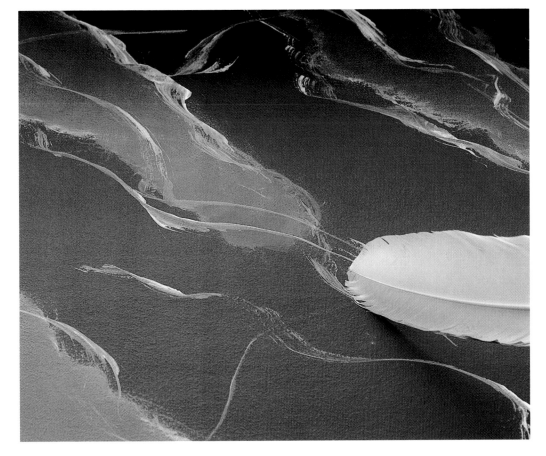

MATERIALS

- White low-luster latex enamel paint, for the base coat.
- White craft acrylic or flat latex paint, for the wash.
- Light gray craft acrylic paint, for the veining.
- Acrylic paint thickener.
- Acrylic paint extender.
- Turkey or pheasant feather.
- Disposable plate.
- High-gloss aerosol clear acrylic sealer.

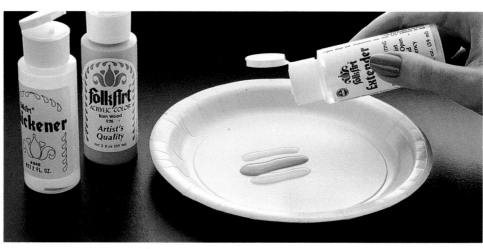

1 Prepare surface (page 16). Apply base coat of white low-luster latex enamel. Allow to dry. Apply a long pool of light gray craft acrylic paint onto disposable plate. Apply a pool of thickener on one side of white paint and extender on the other.

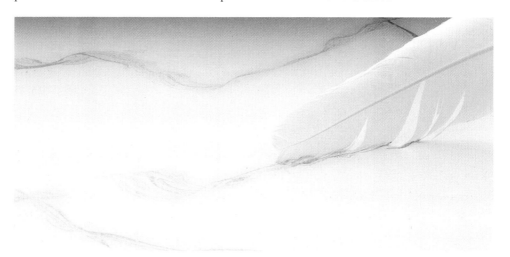

2 Run edge of a feather through pools, picking up some thickener, paint, and extender on feather. Place tip of feather onto surface; drag feather along, fidgeting and turning it slightly in your hand to create veins. Apply veins in a diagonal direction, crisscrossing the veins as desired. The thickener and extender vary the veins so some areas are opaque and some are translucent.

3 Dilute one part white craft acrylic or flat latex paint with one part water, for the wash; brush over surface generously. Before the wash is completely dry, brush the surface diagonally in both directions, using a soft, dry natural-bristle paintbrush, to soften the look.

4 Allow paint to dry. Apply several coats of high-gloss aerosol clear acrylic sealer.

HOW TO APPLY A FAUX BRECCIA PAINT FINISH

MATERIALS

- White low-luster latex enamel paint, for base coat.
- Light gray or medium gray craft acrylic paint, for veining and specking.
- Burnt sienna craft acrylic paint, for the wash.
- Acrylic paint thickener.
- Acrylic paint extender.

- Natural sea sponge; turkey or pheasant feather.
- ½" (1.3 cm) synthetic-bristle flat artist's brush.
- Fine-bristle scrub brush or toothbrush, for specking.
- Disposable plates; small containers.
- High-gloss aerosol clear acrylic sealer.

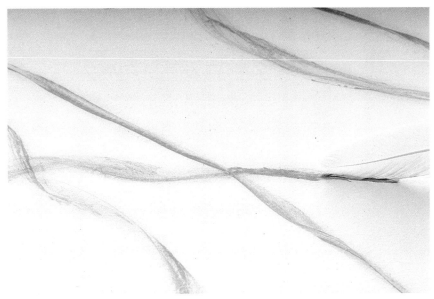

1 Follow step 1, opposite. Following directions for veining in step 2, opposite, apply veins in diagonal direction, crisscrossing them, and leaving football-shaped areas between veins. Allow to dry.

2 Prepare a wash by mixing one part burnt sienna acrylic paint, two parts acrylic extender, and two parts water.

3 Apply the wash to any football-shaped areas between veins, using ½" (1.3 cm) flat artist's brush. Before the wash is completely dry, blot it with a small, dampened sea sponge, to mottle the finish and remove any brush marks. If the wash spreads outside the veins, wipe it off immediately, using a dampened rag.

4 Add a light to moderate amount of specking as on page 91, using diluted gray craft acrylic paint. Allow the paint to dry. Apply several coats of high-gloss aerosol clear acrylic sealer.

FAUX VERDIGRIS

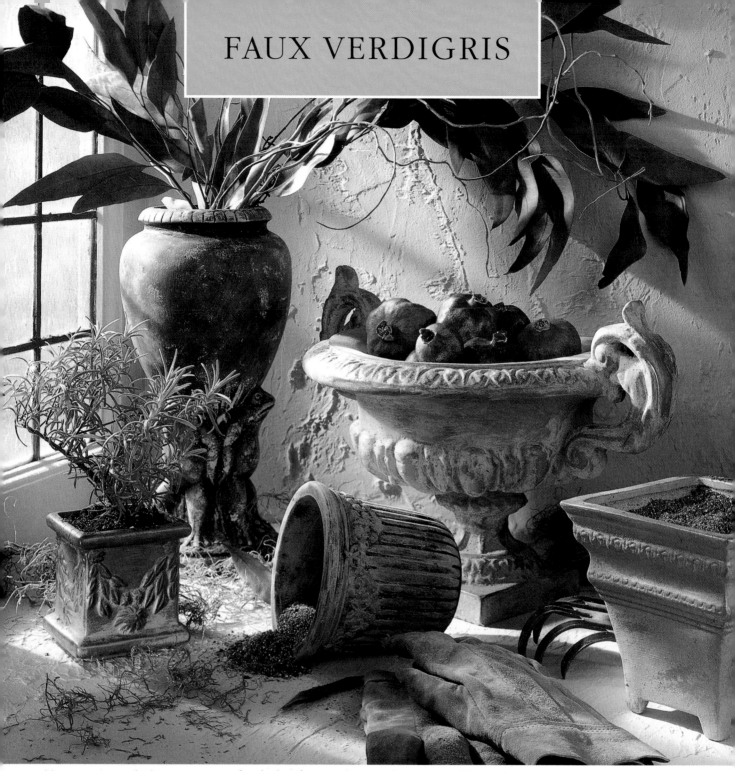

Terra-cotta and plaster pots *are finished in faux verdigris with a variety of black and metallic base coats.*

Faux verdigris is an easy paint finish that has the aged look of tarnished copper, brass, or bronze. Intended for indoor use, faux verdigris works well on cement or plaster statues, and on clay pots with relief designs, for a look as realistic as verdigris pieces of sculpted metal.

To simulate the irregular, weathered appearance of aged metals, a bright aqua paint is applied randomly over a base coat of black or metallic paint. Then a paste made from concrete patching materials and paint is applied, to give added texture and color variation.

In the early stages of verdigris, the aging appears in the recessed areas while the raised areas remain metallic. In faux verdigris, this look is accomplished by using a metallic base coat.

In the advanced stage of verdigris, the recesses have become blackened with age and the raised areas have a weathered appearance due to greenish blue deposits. This look is achieved in faux verdigris by starting with a black base coat.

Metal swing-arm rods
*have a faux verdigris
finish with a bronze
base coat.*

**Plaster, metal, and
wooden accessories**
*(below) have faux
verdigris finishes with
bronze, black, and brass
base coats.*

HOW TO APPLY A FAUX VERDIGRIS PAINT FINISH

MATERIALS

- Flat latex or craft acrylic paint in black or metallic, for the base coat.
- Flat latex or craft acrylic paints in bright aqua and white.
- Dry concrete patch and concrete adhesive, available at hardware stores and builder's supply stores.
- Synthetic paintbrushes.
- Toothbrush.
- Disposable plate and cup.
- Spray bottle, such as a plant sprayer.

VERDIGRIS PASTE

Mix together the following ingredients:

One part bright aqua latex or craft acrylic paint;

Six parts white latex or craft acrylic paint;

Twelve parts dry concrete patch;

Two parts concrete adhesive.

1 Apply an even base coat of black or metallic paint to clean surface, using synthetic paintbrush, making sure paint is applied into any crevices or recessed areas. Allow paint to dry.

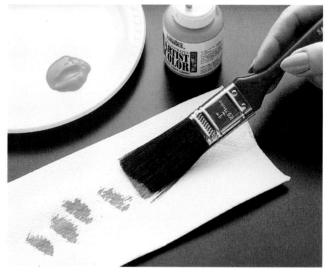

2 Pour small amount of aqua paint onto disposable plate. Thin to a creamy consistency by adding water, if necessary. Dip the tip of the brush into paint; blot on paper towel to remove excess paint.

3 Apply aqua paint randomly with paintbrush in an up-and-down motion called *stippling,* leaving some base coat exposed. Over black base coat, apply aqua paint to raised areas; over metallic base coat, apply aqua paint to flat or recessed areas.

4 Smear aqua paint in some areas, if desired, using a dry paintbrush.

5 Mix the verdigris paste (opposite) in a disposable cup. Using fingers, work the paste into some of the crevices or recessed areas.

6 Spray surface thoroughly with water, using spray bottle, as soon as paste is applied; brush away some paste, if desired, using toothbrush or finger.

7 Drizzle small amount of dry concrete patch over wet areas. Once dry, concrete cannot be removed.

For metallic finishes only. Reapply the metallic paint as necessary to highlight the raised areas. This gives metallics a realistic verdigris appearance, with the more aged aqua areas in the recesses and the shiny, less weathered finish in the raised areas.

A faux rust finish has a timeworn look that complements country, primitive, and contemporary decorating schemes. Finished in faux rust, accessories like lamp bases, picture frames, boxes, vases, candlesticks, and shelf brackets add warm, rustic charm to interiors.

A paste of concrete patching materials and acrylic paints is applied to the surface over a base coat of black paint. For a realistic rusted appearance, use a natural sea sponge to dab paste onto the surface, letting some of the black base coat show. After the paste has dried, sponge paint a light application of burnt sienna craft acrylic paint over the surface.

For the lighter faux rust finish on the horse (opposite), the amounts of the burnt umber and burnt sienna paints in the rust paste were transposed; and, for the sponge-painted top coat, a small amount of yellow oxide craft acrylic paint was mixed into the burnt sienna.

RUST PASTE

Mix together the following ingredients:

One part burnt sienna craft acrylic paint;

Six parts burnt umber craft acrylic paint;

Twelve parts dry concrete patch;

Two parts concrete adhesive.

HOW TO APPLY A FAUX RUST PAINT FINISH

MATERIALS

- Flat latex or craft acrylic paint in black.
- Craft acrylic paints in burnt sienna and burnt umber.
- Dry concrete patch.
- Concrete adhesive.
- Natural sea sponge.
- Disposable cup or bowl.

1 Apply a base coat of black paint, using a synthetic paintbrush. Allow paint to dry.

2 Mix rust paste (above) in disposable cup or bowl. Using a spoon, apply a thin layer of paste onto dampened sea sponge.

3 Smudge the paste onto entire surface, using sponge; allow some of the base coat to show. Then dab with a sea sponge to give a stippled look. Allow to dry.

4 Dip small sea sponge into burnt sienna paint; blot on paper towel. Apply small amount to surface, to brighten rust finish. Allow to dry.

The rich patterns and colors of natural wood grain can be imitated, using a technique that dates back as far as Roman times and was especially popular in the late nineteenth century. Long revered as a technique used exclusively by skilled artisans, wood graining has made a comeback as new tools, such as the wood-graining rocker shown on page 112, have become available. Wood graining is suitable for any smooth surface. Try this painting technique on walls, doors, woodwork, furniture, or trunks.

For faux wood grain, a glaze of latex or craft acrylic paint and paint thickener is applied over a base coat of low-luster latex enamel. The rocker side of a wood-graining tool is dragged through the wet glaze as you rock it back and forth. Each time the tool is rocked, the oval-shaped markings characteristic of pine and other woods are simulated.

The final color of the finish depends on the combined effect of the base coat and the glaze coat. For a natural appearance of wood, a lighter base coat is used with a darker glaze. Suitable colors for the base coat include raw sienna, red oxide, burnt sienna, burnt umber, and beige tones. For the glaze, colors include burnt umber, black, red oxide, and burnt sienna. Because of the wide range of wood stains commonly used on woodwork, it is not necessary to duplicate both the grain and the color of any particular wood.

Become familiar with the techniques by practicing them on a large sheet of cardboard until you can achieve the look of wood. Test the finish before applying it to the actual project.

For the effect of wood parquet, mark the base coat in a grid, such as 4" or 8" (10 or 20.5 cm) squares. You can center the design, or begin at one corner with a full square. Masking off alternate squares in the gridwork, wood-grain the surface in alternating horizontal and vertical directions.

Faux wood grain adds visual interest to the simple chest opposite. It also gives the effect of parquet to the flooring above; a latex enamel paint formulated especially for floors was used for durability.

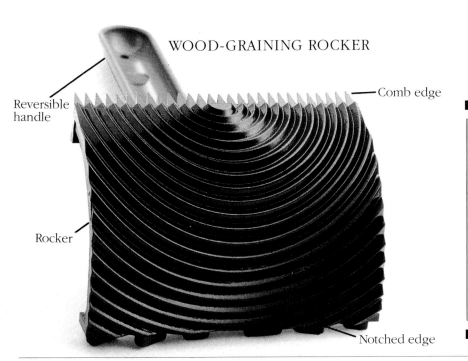

WOOD-GRAINING ROCKER

Reversible handle

Comb edge

Rocker

Notched edge

MATERIALS

- Low-luster latex enamel paint in desired color, for the base coat.
- Craft acrylic paint in desired color or latex paint in desired sheen and color, for the glaze.
- Acrylic paint thickener.
- Satin or high-gloss clear finish or aerosol clear acrylic sealer.

- Wood-graining rocker.
- Paintbrush or paint roller, for applying the base coat.
- Synthetic-bristle paintbrush, for applying the glaze.
- Soft, natural-bristle paintbrush, 3" or 4" (7.5 or 10 cm) wide, for blending the wood-grain effect.
- Straightedge.
- Painter's masking tape, for faux wood parquet finish.

HOW TO PAINT A FAUX WOOD-GRAIN FINISH

1 Prepare surface (page 16). Apply base coat of low-luster latex enamel in desired color, stroking in the desired direction for the wood grain. A paint roller may be used for large areas. Allow to dry.

2 Mix the wood-graining glaze (above). Apply an even coat of glaze over base coat to a small area at a time, stroking in desired direction for wood grain.

3 Slide wood-graining rocker through wet glaze, rocking it slowly to create wood-grain effect. Start at one corner, working in one continuous motion as you slide and rock the tool from one end to another. As you rock the tool, oval markings are created. (Position of rocker corresponds to markings of wood grain, as shown above.)

4 Repeat step 3 for subsequent rows, varying the space between oval markings; wipe excess glaze from tool as necessary. For some rows, pull the comb or notched edge of the wood-graining tool through glaze instead of using rocker; this varies the look by giving a simple, continuous wood grain. A rubber combing tool (page 68) may be used for this step.

5 Brush across surface before glaze is completely dry, using dry, soft, natural-bristle paintbrush, 3" to 4" (7.5 to 10 cm) wide; lightly brush in direction of wood grain, to soften the look. Wipe excess glaze from brush as necessary. Allow the glaze to dry. Apply clear finish or aerosol clear acrylic sealer, if desired.

HOW TO APPLY A FAUX WOOD PARQUET FINISH

1 Apply a base coat as on page 112, step 1. Measure and mark grid on base coat, using straightedge and pencil; center grid or begin with a complete square at one corner.

2 Apply painter's masking tape to alternate squares in grid; use putty knife to trim masking tape diagonally at corners, as shown. Press firmly along the edges of tape, to prevent glaze from seeping through.

3 Mix the wood-graining glaze (page 112). Apply glaze to unmasked squares, using paintbrush in horizontal direction. Slide wood-graining rocker horizontally through the wet glaze on some squares for straight wood-grain effect. Rock the tool horizontally on remaining squares, varying position of oval markings. Work on only a few squares at a time, because glaze dries quickly.

4 Brush across the surface before glaze is completely dry, using dry, soft, natural-bristle paintbrush; lightly brush in direction of wood grain, to soften it. Wipe excess glaze from brush as necessary.

5 Allow paint to dry; remove the masking tape. Apply masking tape over wood-grained squares; apply glaze to unmasked squares, brushing in a vertical direction. Repeat steps 3 and 4 in vertical direction. Allow to dry; remove masking tape. Apply clear finish or aerosol clear acrylic sealer, if desired.

COLOR EFFECTS

Various wood tones, resembling common wood stains such as cherry, honey oak, and walnut, can be created, depending on the paint colors selected for the base coat and the glaze.

Cherry stain is duplicated by using a dark rust base coat and a burnt umber glaze.

Honey oak is duplicated by using a light tan base coat and a golden tan glaze.

Walnut stain is duplicated by using a dark gold base coat and a burnt umber glaze.

FAUX MOIRÉ

For the watermarked look of silk moiré taffeta, use a process similar to the wood-graining technique of faux wood. The subtle tone-on-tone pattern can be created in any color for a coordinated decorating scheme. This finish is recommended for small areas, such as below a chair rail or within frame moldings.

The rocker tool designed for wood graining (page 112) is also used for this watermarked effect. A paint glaze (opposite) is applied over a base coat of paint, and the graining tool is pulled and rocked through the glaze to create impressions. Then a dry paintbrush is pulled across the markings to mimic the crosswise grain of moiré.

The glaze used for faux moiré contains more paint than most glazes, making it thicker and more opaque. In order to finish the graining before the glaze has dried, apply the glaze to a small area at a time. If faux moiré is used on the wall area below a chair rail or border, work from the chair rail to the baseboard in 12" (30.5 cm) sections, working quickly.

Unlike faux wood, moiré is simulated by using a darker shade for the base coat and a lighter glaze for the top coat. This gives the brighter sheen that is characteristic of moiré fabric.

HOW TO APPLY A FAUX MOIRÉ PAINT FINISH

MATERIALS

- Low-luster latex enamel paint in darker shade, for base coat.
- Low-luster latex enamel paint in lighter shade, for glaze; or base-coat paint, lightened with white paint, may be used.
- Latex paint conditioner, such as Floetrol®.
- Wood-graining rocker.
- Paint roller or paintbrush, for applying the base coat and the glaze.
- Natural-bristle paintbrush, 2" to 3" (5 to 7.5 cm) wide, for dry brushing.

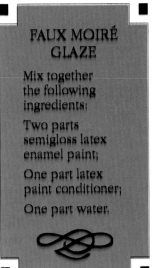

FAUX MOIRÉ GLAZE

Mix together the following ingredients:

Two parts semigloss latex enamel paint;

One part latex paint conditioner;

One part water.

1 Prepare surface and apply base coat of low-luster latex enamel as on page 112, step 1; use darker shade for base coat.

2 Mix glaze (left). Apply an even coat of glaze over base coat to a small area at a time, rolling or brushing vertically.

3 Slide graining tool vertically through wet glaze, occasionally rocking it slowly back and forth as shown on page 113, to create watermarked effect. Start at one corner, working in one continuous motion as you slide and rock the tool from one end to another. As you rock the tool, oval markings are created.

4 Repeat step 3 for subsequent rows; stagger the oval markings, and work quickly before glaze dries. Wipe excess glaze from tool.

5 Pull dry brush horizontally across surface when glaze has partially dried, using a natural-bristle paintbrush; this mimics the crosswise grain of the moiré fabric. Wipe excess glaze from the brush as necessary. Allow paint to dry.

Combining Techniques

COORDINATING PAINT FINISHES

As you decorate your home, you may combine several painting techniques. For example, use paint finishes that have an aged look in a country room, or those that give a look of elegance in a traditional room. For a dramatic effect, you can boldly mix colors, patterns, and textures throughout the room. You may even want to combine two or more paint finishes in a single piece.

Traditional room (left) features rich faux finishes that look like their real counterparts. The moiré finish (page 116) on the wall creates a backdrop resembling silk moiré taffeta. The alabaster finish (page 102) on the sconce and chair rail portrays the elegance of marble. The verdigris finish (page 104) of the frame and candlesticks has the warmth and texture of aged bronze and brass.

Contemporary room (below) combines creative and colorful patterns for a free expression of style. Sponge painting (page 78) adds a mottled allover pattern to the walls. The swirled designs (page 33) are painted following a few easy steps, and the diagonal stripes on the picture frame are painted using the technique for guided designs (page 29). Combing techniques (page 68) are used to finish the widemouth vase.

Country room (left) has an interesting mix of rustic and aged looks. The walls are color washed (page 82) for a worn effect. The hutch, which is both stenciled (page 44) and antiqued (page 84), holds several accessories with a faux rust finish (page 108) and a fabric placemat that is sponge painted (page 78). Next to the hutch is a stenciled antique chair.

COMBINING TECHNIQUES

Glaze finishes (page 65) are combined to decorate this small jewelry box. The top and sides of the box are sponge painted; from top to bottom, the drawers are painted using the ragging-on, texturizing, and combing techniques.

Faux finishes are used for the planter below, with onyx (page 100) for the borders and verdigris (page 104) for the center area.

Faux mosaic, stamped over color washing, gives the walls a rich, textural effect. First apply the color wash (page 82), then the faux mosaic design (page 93).

MORE IDEAS FOR COMBINING TECHNIQUES

Headboard has decoupage designs (page 52), applied over color washing (page 82); the spindled posts are sponge painted (page 78).

Contemporary table combines three paint finishes. Faux granite (page 88) and faux alabaster (page 102) are used for the tabletop, and faux rust (page 108) for the legs. For a blended color scheme, faux alabaster is also used for the vase and colors related to the faux granite are used for the color-washed finish (page 82).

Wall display (above) features a shelf with freehand designs (page 40) and stenciled wall designs (page 44). The ceramics are decorated with freehand designs combined with sponge painting (page 78); specialty ceramic paints (page 60) were used.

INDEX

CREDITS

COWLES
Creative Publishing

President: Iain Macfarlane

DECORATIVE PAINTING
Created by: The Editors of
Cowles Creative Publishing, Inc.

Books available in this series:
*Bedroom Decorating, Creative Window
Treatments, Decorating for Christmas,
Decorating the Living Room, Creative
Accessories for the Home, Decorating
with Silk & Dried Flowers, Kitchen &
Bathroom Ideas, Decorating the Kitchen,
Decorative Painting, Decorating Your
Home for Christmas, Decorating for
Dining & Entertaining, Decorating with
Fabric & Wallcovering, Decorating the
Bathroom, Decorating with Great Finds,
Affordable Decorating, Picture-Perfect
Walls, More Creative Window
Treatments, Outdoor Decor, The Gift of
Christmas, Home Accents in a Flash,
Painted Illusions*

Group Executive Editor: Zoe A. Graul
Senior Technical Director: Rita C. Arndt
Senior Project Manager: Joseph Cella
Project Manager: Tracy Stanley
Senior Art Director: Lisa Rosenthal
Art Director: Stephanie Michaud
Writer: Rita C. Arndt
Editor: Janice Cauley
Researcher/Designer: Michael Basler
Research Assistant: Linda Neubauer
Sample Supervisor: Carol Olson
Senior Technical Photo Stylist:
  Bridget Haugh
Technical Photo Stylist: Susan Pasqual
Styling Director: Bobbette Destiche
Crafts Stylists: Coralie Sathre,
  Joanne Wawra
Assistant Crafts Stylist: Deanna Despard
Artisans: Corliss Forstrom,
  Phyllis Galbraith, Linda Neubauer,
  Carol Pilot, Nancy Sundeen
*Vice President of Development Planning
  & Production:* Jim Bindas
Director of Photography: Mike Parker
Creative Photo Coordinator:
  Cathleen Shannon
Studio Manager: Marcia Chambers
Lead Photographer: Mark Macemon
Photographers: Stuart Block,
  Rebecca Hawthorne, Mike Hehner,
  Rex Irmen, Bill Lindner, Paul Najlis,
  Charles Nields, Mike Parker,
  Robert Powers
Contributing Photographers:
  Howard Kaplan, Paul Markert,
  Brad Parker

Production Manager: Amelia Merz
Senior Desktop Publishing Specialist:
  Joe Fahey
Production Staff: Mike Hehner,
  Janet Morgan, Robert Powers,
  Mike Schauer, Kay Wethern,
  Nik Wogstad
Shop Supervisor: Phil Juntti
Scenic Carpenters: John Nadeau,
  Mike Peterson, Greg Wallace
Consultants: Carolynne Darling,
  Nadine Millot, Kathy Tilton
Contributors: American Art Clay Co.,
  Inc.; Art Cast; Daubert Coated
  Products, Inc.; Decart, Inc.; Deco
  Art; Dee-Signs Stencils; Duncan
  Enterprises; Fabby Custom Lighting;
  Flood Company; Folk Art; Fuller
  O'Brien Paints; House Parts; Plaid
  Enterprises; Symphony Fine Art
  Instruments; Waverly, Division of
  F. Schumacher & Co.
Printed on American paper by:
  World Color

00 99 98 97 / 5 4 3 2

Cowles Creative Publishing, Inc. offers
a variety of how-to books. For
information write:
  Cowles Creative Publishing
  Subscriber Books
  5900 Green Oak Drive
  Minnetonka, MN 55343